SIMPLIFY

Entertaining

A **Reader's Digest Simpler Life**™ Book

Designed, edited, and produced by Weldon Owen

THE READER'S DIGEST ASSOCIATION, INC.

Executive Editor, Trade Books Joseph Gonzalez
Senior Design Director, Trade Books Henrietta Stern
Project Editor Candace Conard
Project Art Director Jane Wilson

WELDON OWEN INC.

President John Owen
Publisher Roger S. Shaw
Series Editor Janet Goldenberg
Managing Editor Dianne Jacob
Contributing Editor Vicki Webster
Copy Editors Lisa R. Bornstein, Gail Nelson

Art Director Emma Forge
Senior Designer Elizabeth Marken
Production Designer Brynn Breuner
Design Assistant William Erik Evans
Icon Illustrator Matt Graif

Production Director Stephanie Sherman
Production Manager Jen Dalton

Project Photographers Chris Shorten, Brian Pierce
Photo Stylist JoAnn Masaoka Van Atta
Photo Editor Anne Stovell

A Reader's Digest/Weldon Owen Publication
Copyright © 1998 The Reader's Digest Association, Inc., and Weldon Owen Inc.

Library of Congress Cataloging in Publication Data
Barber, Mary Corpening, 1969–
    Simplify entertaining / Mary Corpening Barber & Sara Corpening.
        p.   cm.
    Includes index.
    ISBN 0-7621-0064-8
    1. Entertaining.   2. Cookery.   I. Corpening, Sara, 1969–
II. Title.
TX731.B353   1998
642'.4—dc21   98-9189

Printed in China

*A note on weights and measures: Metric equivalences given for
U.S. weights and measures are approximate. Actual equivalences may vary.*

SIMPLIFY
Entertaining

MARY BARBER & SARA CORPENING
WITH LORI LYN NARLOCK

Illustrations by JEFF MOORES

The Reader's Digest Association, Inc.
Pleasantville, New York/Montreal

CONTENTS

If you're at ease when preparing for your party,
your mood is sure to rub off on your guests.

ENJOYING YOUR OWN PARTY

* —— ✳ —— *

Simplify entertaining? Are we kidding? No! It's true: You can throw great parties—and enjoy them as much as your guests do—without putting your life on hold, slaving in the kitchen for weeks, or ransacking your bank account.

We know entertaining can be simple because we've been throwing easy, fun parties ever since we were toddlers. Our parents entertained a steady stream of guests in our North Carolina home, and we helped with everything from elegant dinner parties to impromptu backyard barbecues. Our parents served our early culinary efforts with great pride, and we observed that if the cookies were a little burned or if the salad dressing had a tad too much vinegar, no one seemed to notice—they were too busy having a good time.

Our parents instilled in us not only a love of entertaining, but also the confidence that lets us relax and enjoy our own creations when we cater private parties in the San Francisco Bay area. That confidence, we have discovered, is the true secret behind successful entertaining.

Easier said than done, you might say. And there is no denying that part of being a relaxed host or hostess comes with practice. But what is even more important is simply knowing how to get the maximum result from minimum effort—and that's what *Simplify Entertaining* is all about.

Our book is filled with the many ideas and techniques that we've developed over the years—both in our social lives and as professional caterers—to help you make the most of your time, talent, and budget. Everything it takes to orchestrate a successful gathering—large or small, formal or casual—is included, whether it's preparing a one-pot meal, disguising tired furniture, or creating a lively party atmosphere.

Helpful pointers also explain how every would-be host or hostess can concentrate on what really matters to the success of a party and eliminate all the rest of the fuss and bother. Throughout this book, we'll show you the time-saving techniques that the professionals rely on to plan stylish parties that are exciting, fun—and simple—from beginning to end.

As you use *Simplify Entertaining*, you will gain something beyond mere style and technique: the self-assurance that will enable you to create parties that your guests will feel honored and excited to attend. You'll also come to appreciate the fact that graciousness and enthusiasm will overshadow clutter in the kitchen, dust on the shelves, or burned cookies. In short, you will learn just how easy it is to enjoy planning, preparing, and attending your own parties.

Mary Corpening Barber   *Sara Corpening*

A relaxed, confident approach is the simple
secret to successful entertaining.

SIMPLE SYMBOLS

S CATTERED THROUGHOUT *Simplify Entertaining* you'll find a series of colorful tip boxes. Each one contains easy-to-follow advice to help you save time, money, and energy—all those things that generate stress when in short supply. Using these realistic and fun ideas, you can create an effect that appears far more grand than the effort that goes into it. Watch for these symbols and the great ideas that follow:

 Labor Savers feature hints for easing the burden of planning a party without sacrificing results. When it seems that there is just too much work to be done, turn to these ideas to find out how you can delegate jobs and share certain responsibilities.

 Stress Busters show simple, surefire methods for reducing the pressure of party planning. Take good note of these stress-reducing tips so that when you finally open the door to greet your guests, you will be cool, calm, and collected.

 Time Savers can help when it seems as though a thousand things are clamoring for your attention. Refer to these timely tips to cut minutes, even hours, from your schedule without cutting any corners on style, elegance, or enjoyment.

 Cost Cutters offer proof that you can create a sense of occasion with plenty of style and for very little cash (and sometimes for none at all). When you rely on these thrifty, budget-saving ideas, none of your guests will suspect you're economizing.

 Bright Ideas will surprise you with all manner of innovative and imaginative suggestions for easy entertaining with flair. Follow the advice that you'll find here—or just use these tips as springboards for your own brand of creativity.

 Rules of Thumb take all the mystery out of estimating quantities such as how many glasses you'll need, how much wine to buy, and whether the amount of available space at your party site will be too little, too much, or just right.

 Simply Safer tips are practical recommendations for ways to remain safety-conscious when throwing a party. Dangers lurk in any situation where crowds gather and food and drink is served. These ideas present a few simple strategies that you can implement easily to protect both you and your guests.

 Don't Forget reminders keep you focused as you organize your party, regardless of the size or formality of the event. This advice puts the essentials at your fingertips. And when your party is in motion and having fun is uppermost, refer to these strategies to keep everything running smoothly.

MAKE core
DECISIONS Now

—✳—

1 Decide the **how, where,** and **when** well in advance to keep stress low and the chances of success high. **2** Declare that you will **have fun.** **3** Choose only those occasions worth commemorating with a party, so you'll **feel excited** about what lies ahead. **4** Be truthful about whether you **feel comfortable** having business associates come to your home. You might be more relaxed at a restaurant. **5** Select an **appropriate site** for the number of people—a small group in a large hall can feel overwhelming. **6** Find a date that's free of other events with **ample time** beforehand. **7** During the holidays, consider an informal **weekday gathering** to avoid competing with company parties or galas. **8** Try for **balance** among your guests: Seat women next to men, introverts next to extroverts. **9** Approach a theme **playfully** and invite your guests to play along; they will talk about the fun they had for months to come, and you'll revel in your success. ●

PLANNING THE PERFECT PARTY

ENJOYING THE FUN FROM DAY ONE

———✳———

Whether you entertain only a few times a year or throw parties all the time, you probably wish you could spend less time working at entertaining and more time enjoying your friends and relatives. Well, there's good news: You can.

Like any successful endeavor, a good party—especially a simple one—takes planning. But that's where the fun starts. Kick into fantasy gear. Pull a great celebration out of your memory archives and relive it, drink by drink and dance by dance. Think about what you enjoyed most. Or create an original party in your mind. Picture the location, the mood, the guests' attire. Let these fantasies and ideas form a springboard for decisions you can make now.

Enjoy making your guest list. This is your opportunity to invite your favorite people and to create an interesting mix of guests. Remember, there's really no truly "perfect" party—just one that works perfectly for you.

WHAT'S THE OCCASION?

*

A PARTY IS ITS OWN REASON FOR BEING: WE ALL NEED TO BE SOCIAL. BUT WE ALSO NEED TO CELEBRATE LIFE'S EVENTS, AND THEY'RE COUNTLESS, FROM THE MOMENTOUS TO THE MUNDANE.

The occasions worth commemorating with a party are the ones that excite you. When you love what you're doing, or love the reason you're doing it, you will exude confidence and style, and people will notice. Your efforts will be fun, not a series of chores to get through, and you and your guests will remember the event for a long time. On the other hand, if you just can't work up the enthusiasm to have the gang over for the Super Bowl, or host your spouse's boss, or cook dinner for that nice new couple down the hall, let it wait.

A special event *such as an anniversary can be the catalyst for your party. You might ask the couple of honor to take the limelight and dance to their favorite song.*

When the party spirit demands to be heard, you will know it's time to put out a spread and summon the crowds.

MAKING HOLIDAYS EASY

Holidays are traditional times for feasting and frolicking. For some of us, they're the only times in the year when we entertain family and friends. That's all the more reason to simplify the party-giving process.

Consider the following no-fuss ideas for making special days distinctive:

For a simple New Year's Eve party, invite friends to watch the countdown to midnight on television. Serve champagne and a few easy snacks—assorted cheeses, smoked salmon, and sliced pumpernickel.

On February 14th, serve your Valentine a romantic dinner in bed with soft music and subdued lighting. Try a tray of take-out sushi, sake, and, for a passionate dessert, heart-shaped chocolate cookies.

Make your mother a star on her day: Invite her over for a breakfast of just-from-the-oven muffins (use a mix), fruit, and fresh-squeezed juice, with her grandchildren playing waiters.

For Father's Day, take Dad out to the ball game and treat him to hot dogs, peanuts, and the best seats you can afford.

Even if your house is the family's destination for holiday revelry, you needn't play galley slave. Ask relatives to bring no-cook ingredients for Easter lunch. At Thanksgiving, delegate dinner: Assign

If you can't work up the enthusiasm to have the gang over— wait. When the party spirit moves you, you'll know it's time to summon the crowds.

everyone a dish, from appetizers to dessert. Or buy prepared side dishes and serve them on your own decorative plates.

ATTENTION TO PURPOSE

Let the occasion dictate the format of your party. Host an evening reception to announce an engagement, an afternoon tea for an expectant mother, a festive dinner to mark a personal triumph, such as a marathon won, a bar exam passed, a new career launched. A ceremonial lunch can honor the new graduate, whether

Eliminate Last-Minute Stresses

If you have an extended family that rotates the hosting of holiday gatherings, plan ahead. Set a date in January to meet, and schedule and assign the year's celebrations in advance. Whether you confer by phone or use the meeting as an excuse for another family get-together, you'll avoid the stress of last-minute arrangements.

from high school, college, or a vocational training course. Commemorate a retirement with after-dinner cigars and brandy. Host an elegant brunch for a wedding shower. Observe a monumental birthday—13th, 18th, 21st, 30th, 40th, 50th, 75th—with a rooftop supper. Celebrate a benchmark wedding anniversary with a midday garden party.

Less majestic events deserve equal notice but can be celebrated on a simpler, less expensive basis. On your neighbor's moving day, show up with a movable feast of sandwiches and finger food and spread it out on the packing crates. Honor the first day of school with a hamburger dinner in the park. Send off international vacationers with a delicious sampling of hors d'oeuvres from around the world. When visitors arrive from out of town, salute them with a picnic and invite a handful of friends to join you.

A public park *can be a welcome change from a restaurant as a stage for celebrating a birthday, an anniversary, or a personal triumph.*

If your party has a guest of honor, capture the day for him or her with sentimental messages. Compile a book of memories written by friends and encourage them to record their personal recollections of happy times spent together; or hang butcher paper on the wall and ask everyone to

After a productive Saturday, reward yourself by asking friends over for a serve-yourself dessert party of ice cream and toppings.

write a message. Designate a party photographer, put the resulting pictures in an album, and present it to the guest of honor. Package servings of the food in festive take-out containers and send the honoree home with a second dinner. The more personal that you make the occasion, the more honored your special guest

will feel. Your efforts needn't be elaborate or expensive: a heartfelt toast can forge a strong bond that will last a lifetime.

IMPROMPTU FUN

Don't overlook the pleasures of a spontaneous gathering. When you are craving company, be impulsive. Invite neighbors over; order sandwich fixings or a couple of pizzas and have them delivered. Then put out a selection of cold microbrews and sodas, set the table for easy self-service— and let the good times roll.

If you need more inspiration for entertaining, turn an ordinary occurrence into an occasion. Monday-night football provides the perfect excuse for serving up hot chili and cold beer. Televised awards shows like the Oscars or the Emmys offer you a chance to visit with friends over a light dinner and good wine. Or, after a productive Saturday afternoon, reward yourself by asking a couple of friends (and their kids) over for a serve-yourself dessert party of ice cream and toppings.

BUSINESS ENTERTAINING
WITH FLAIR

✳

INTERACTING WITH MANAGERS, CLIENTS, AND COWORKERS IS AN IMPORTANT PART OF PROFESSIONAL LIFE. IN SOME CAREERS, ENTERTAINING COLLEAGUES IS MANDATORY FOR THOSE WHO WANT TO SUCCEED.

In other professions, it's simply an easy way to make vital but unchosen relationships flow more smoothly.

Either way, you can enjoy a business get-together as much as any other kind. Just make a few decisions up front: Will this be a business meeting or simply a social gathering of business colleagues? Whom will you invite? How long would you like the gathering to last? What do you want to achieve by wining and dining these particular people?

Next, ask yourself how well you know your business associates and how far you want to draw them into your personal life. For example, do you want them to see your home? Your housekeeping skills and your surroundings—furniture, books, pictures, family, pets—reveal a lot more about you than the few snapshots tacked to the wall of your office cubicle.

STAYING SANE

To emphasize the professional nature of a business-related event, hold it during the week. If a meal is involved, start the meeting early, for example at about 7:00 A.M. for breakfast, 11:30 A.M. for lunch, and

Decide whether you'll hold a business or social gathering, and
be sure to make your decision clear to your guests.

5:30 P.M. for dinner. These times allow you to finish at a reasonable hour and to beat the crowds if you're meeting in a public place. If you rent a hotel room, ask for blackboards, easels, slide projectors, and other equipment. Invite only those people involved in the business at hand. Extend invitations by phone, and ask each guest to confirm the day before the meeting. If you stay at your workplace and order in food, be sure to put a large "Do Not Disturb" sign on the door.

Regardless of whether you or your company will be paying for the event, set a budget and decide on a method of payment. To avoid awkward situations, prepay the caterer, restaurant, or service staff. On the day of the meeting, have a credit card on hand and enough cash to pay for such incidental expenses as coat checking, valet parking, or a bar tab.

A business party needn't be lavish. When you're entertaining people who can influence your career, it's safer to be restrained.

For a purely social gathering of business cohorts, a restaurant or a rented room provides the least stressful venue. If you choose to entertain at home, hire reliable help so you'll be free to mingle (and, not incidentally, to appear at your relaxed best). With no business on the agenda, no day of the week is out-of-bounds. Friday or Saturday evening will work as well as a weeknight. Still, make sure you start the evening early and limit the length

A restaurant *is a great place for a purely social gathering of coworkers. Meet for lunch, after-work drinks, or dinner and include spouses and significant others.*

of the event: For a cocktail party, two hours is sufficient. If you're having dinner and drinks, allow three to four hours.

INCLUDING OTHERS

Include spouses and significant others when you're entertaining for business pleasure rather than as a business obligation. In fact, include anyone who might be offended if left out. When your career is involved, you shouldn't ignore anyone. If you have time, send written or printed invitations; otherwise, a phone call will do for all but the most formal parties.

Above all, relax and don't overdo it. Remember that a business party, even for the top brass, needn't be lavish—quite the contrary. When you're entertaining people who can influence your career, it's generally safer to be restrained.

By now some of your colleagues have probably become your friends. Entertain them as you would anyone else in your nonworking life, either by themselves or with other friends and family.

MAKING ARRANGEMENTS

—✳—

YOU'LL WANT TO MAKE CERTAIN DECISIONS NOW TO ENSURE THAT YOU CAN HAVE THE KIND OF PARTY YOU DESIRE. CHOOSING THE LOCATION AND DATE AND CREATING THE GUEST LIST ARE TASKS BETTER DONE SOONER THAN LATER.

How do you choose just the right spot for your get-together? The possibilities are endless, from private clubs to public parks, from a fashionable four-star restaurant to the neighborhood hot-dog stand.

Where you entertain depends on such factors as the theme or nature of the occasion; how much money you want to dole out; how much time you want your guests to spend getting there; whom you're entertaining; the size of your group; and how much noise your guests will be making—or will want to be shielded from.

Often, the simplest, most comfortable place to entertain—and usually the least expensive—is your home. For a small group, confine the party to one or two rooms by arranging the furniture and refreshments there. Close the doors to off-limits areas. For a large crowd, open as many rooms as you can and move furniture to create open paths and ease traffic flow. If it's warm and weather permits, open the doors to the outside and let your party spread out onto the lawn, into the garden, or onto the deck.

If you'll be entertaining outdoors, find a spot with sufficient shelter in case the weather changes.

If your home won't work, there are plenty of other options. In fact, researching great party locations can be part of the fun—and in the process, you'll build a resource bank to draw on for future events.

First, decide the kind of place you're looking for: a quiet retreat for your office conference, a glamorous backdrop for your parents' anniversary dinner, or a child-proof spot for an eighth birthday romp. To help kick your imagination into high gear, peruse the home-design, garden, and cooking sections of magazines for inspiration. Pick up a travel guide to your area. You might find a park, historic house, grand hotel, or quaint bed-and-breakfast that would be perfect for your party. Search the local papers and the Internet.

A community hall *or other local venue can be transformed into a wonderful party space. Their facilities often include a kitchen as well as pots and pans, tables, and chairs.*

Ask friends for ideas or reports on great places where they've attended events in the past. Find resources in the phone book under party and event planners, party-gear rental companies, and caterers. These companies may be able to rent you just the venue you want—with or without their particular services.

Make a list of possible sites. When speaking with the person who manages the rental of the site, determine whether

A location that provides built-in entertainment is an easy way to offer your guests an unusual and unforgettable experience.

the site meets such basic criteria as price, hours of availability, and capacity. Be careful not to choose a space that's too large. A few too many people in a small room can feel cozy; a small group in too large a space can feel overwhelming. Ask these questions: Are food and alcohol allowed? Does the space have its own caterers and other services or will you be permitted to provide your own? What, if any, parking facilities exist? How accessible is the site? How many entrances are there? Does it have stairways or elevators?

Once you've found a spot that seems to meet your needs, make an inspection visit. Check lighting, kitchen facilities, rest rooms, space for dancing or games, and whether there are enough electrical outlets. Ask what changes can be made to the space's furnishings or configuration. Make sure that nearby neighbors won't be

THE RIGHT RESTAURANT

SELECTING A PUBLIC EATERY for your event is simple if you develop criteria before you start. Decide what type of atmosphere you'd like—quiet, formal, fun, ethnic, or trendy. Set a time for brunch, lunch, or dinner. Next, set a budget and stick to it.

Simple

Look in the review section of local magazines and newspapers for new and well-received spots. Reviews will also provide basic information such as atmosphere, service, prices, and hours.

Simpler

Check the Yellow Pages of your phone book. Call around and select one or two sites. Visit each to examine the menu, check the atmosphere, and investigate the amenities.

Simplest

Patronize a restaurant that you or a trusted friend already know and like. It will give you confidence and reduce stress. If you are a regular customer, your business will be more valued.

---

disturbed by the traffic or noise from your party—especially if it's an evening event.

Pick a site that suits the nature of the occasion and your tastes or those of your guest of honor. A location that provides built-in amusement or entertainment can offer your guests an unusual and unforgettable experience. These days party venues go far beyond the typical rental hall.

Consider these ideas: Hold a formal cocktail party or dinner in a favorite museum or art gallery. Arrange a private tour and tasting at a winery or brewery. Hold your child's next birthday party at the aquarium. Gather friends at a cooking school to make dinner for a bride- and groom-to-be. Throw a teenage birthday party at a bowling alley. Host a wedding shower or birthday party at a pottery studio. Invite colleagues to a rock-climbing school for a team-building party.

If you've fallen in love with a location that's not exactly perfect, don't despair. A little imagination and a few simple props can work wonders. Is the room too austere or unattractive? Play set designer. Haul in potted plants, pictures, and spotlights. Is the space too small for your group? Hold an open house, where people will come and go in smaller groups. Or move furniture out of the room to make more space. Is the room too large? Carve it into smaller spaces by setting up screens and arranging furniture in intimate groupings.

THE GREAT OUTDOORS

Often an outdoor site provides the best atmosphere of all. Throw a romantic party on the water aboard a yacht or sailboat. Go to a racetrack for a bachelor or bachelorette party. Hold an Easter-egg hunt with friends at a country club. Kids and

Personal Space

For maximum traffic flow and interaction, marry the number of guests to the size of the location. Calculate the area of empty floor space in each room and divide by the number of guests; allow about 16 square feet (1.5m²) per person.

grown-ups alike will love a graduation party at the zoo. Have a pool party at a public swimming pool.

Outdoor events require a little creative planning. If you'll be entertaining out-of-doors, look for sufficient shelter in case the weather changes. Erect a tent or a temporary overhang to foil unexpected showers. To provide shade on a hot, sunny day, set up colorful market umbrellas. When you can't depend on balmy temperatures, rent portable heaters. If you're entertaining in

a remote area, rent a van or bus to shuttle guests to and from the site. For rustic or out-of-the-way locations, rent portable toilets, and bring food, camp chairs, and blankets for sitting on and keeping warm.

EASY RESTAURANTS

A local eatery—from a fine dining room to a casual bistro—lets you celebrate at the level of formality you choose. And a restaurant is one of the most stress-free, least time-consuming places to entertain. When you've chosen a restaurant and made the reservation, pay a visit to select a table that will allow you privacy and quiet. For a large group, request a private room or a space secluded from the main dining room. Introduce yourself to the manager and, if possible, to the chef who will be on duty. Discuss dietary restrictions and ask to taste dishes you are considering for your gathering. Select a menu that allows

Leave the work *to someone else. Choose a friendly bistro or café where you can relax with friends without blowing your budget.*

one or two choices for each course. Ask about any potential hidden costs, including corkage, cake slicing, and gratuities. Arrange to pay the bill before the event; that way you will prevent awkward wrangling over the check during the party.

THE RIGHT DATE

Face it: Everyone's calendar is booked solid. In today's fast-paced world, it's all but impossible to find a block of free time. So how do you pick a day that's right for everybody?

You don't. Simply select a day when there are no dental appointments, Little League games, or important afternoon business meetings scheduled—and the evening is open. Having the afternoon free of other obligations gives you more time and energy to prepare for the party.

National holidays are easy, because you know about them well ahead of time and sometimes have an extra day or two off work to prepare. During the Christmas holidays, consider arranging an informal weekday gathering to avoid competing with company parties, charity functions, and other lavish weekend affairs.

What about milestone birthdays or anniversaries that fall midweek? Hold the big celebration on a weekend close to the event—after, if possible, to build up anticipation. Honor the day itself with a simple but memorable gesture such as an elegant bouquet of flowers, a well-chosen gift, and a quiet dinner.

The day of the week sets the mood and the attitude for your party. Sunday through Thursday—school and work

Holidays Are Doable

If you must choose a date that competes with other events, such as the Saturday night of a holiday weekend, give your guests at least a month's advance notice and request that they reserve the date. Follow up later with a detailed invitation, either written or phoned, confirming that date and conveying time and place.

nights—call for earlier, quieter affairs. If you don't have to get up early the next morning, you're more likely to relax and enjoy yourself. Friday evening is great for a kick-off-your-shoes get-together with the gang. For a large party or a sit-down dinner, aim for a Saturday night. You'll have more time to prepare, and your guests can relax and let loose.

Summer and holiday events may be less stressful and more successful if held during the week. Many people go away for long weekends during the summer, so Thursday night may be your best bet to catch them in town.

TIMING IS EVERYTHING

No matter when you schedule your party, someone is bound to arrive just as you're stepping out of the shower, and the rest of your guests will show up half an hour late. Plan ahead by having a designated greeter ready and waiting well before party time, and have chilled drinks and snacks on hand for any early arrivals.

Unless your friends are early birds, reserve breakfast parties for business. A decent hour for brunch is 11:00 A.M. Start lunch at noon. An afternoon party that doesn't include a meal usually takes place between 2:00 and 5:00 P.M.

Begin a cocktail party at 6:00 P.M., and if you're not serving dinner, end the party at 8:00. This type of party works well during the week, when guests face early wake-up calls the next day. For a party that includes dinner, start cocktails at 7:00 and dinner no later than 8:00. If children will be present, start as early as 6:00, with cocktails for the adults and dinner for the kids. For an after-dinner party, invite guests to arrive after 8:30.

Sometimes guests do not arrive in time for the main attraction. Don't wait. Greet the latecomers, see that they are served, and introduce them to the conversation or activity taking place. If someone arrives after a meal has been eaten, simply reheat leftovers for them, or keep a small plate of snacks handy. Not even the latest arrival deserves to go hungry.

If you want your party to end at a designated time, say so when you extend the invitations. If you want the last straggling guests to depart and they haven't,

If an unexpected guest shows up, set another place at the table. People will remember how well you handled an awkward situation.

enlist a friend to drop the hint by exclaiming how late it is and heading for the door. If stragglers still linger, you may have to tell them it's time to go—gently.

Sometimes unforeseeable crises occur and you might have to reschedule or cancel a party. There are a few ways to do so. The first is to pick a new date and simply call invited guests, helpers, and any other vendors to inform them of the change. It is also perfectly acceptable to cancel a party altogether, as long as you reach everybody to let them know. Obviously, one should do so as early as possible.

If you need to reschedule or cancel a large party and you have already hired vendors or reserved a restaurant, be sure to read through contracts and cancellation policies for any possible fees that may be incurred. If you are rescheduling, most service providers are unlikely to penalize you for setting a different date.

Open-House Parties Throw Themselves

An open house is perhaps the most carefree kind of party to host—especially during the busy holidays. Guests can come and go at their convenience, and you can take more time to visit with each guest while avoiding the stress and effort of staging a multicourse feast. Simply lay out an assortment of self-serve snacks that can stay at room temperature for a few hours.

A diverse guest list helps make
a party interesting.

THE GUEST LIST

Unless you're holding a business event or hosting a party for someone else, there's only one reason to invite people: You like them. But when in doubt about whether to invite a person you don't particularly care for, choose the least stressful option. Remember that it's sometimes easier to invite someone than not.

So, in your mind, gather the people with whom you want to spend time. Then make a list of the people you would like to entertain. Match the head count to your budget, the occasion, and the capacity of your home or the party venue.

How many guests should you invite? An elegant sit-down dinner takes a lot of preparation, so keep the number low. Between 6 and 10 is good. A holiday cookie exchange, pumpkin-carving party, or buffet supper can suit a medium-size group of 10 to 15. An outdoor barbecue or potluck in a park can accommodate a crowd of 15 or more. These numbers are only guidelines: If you feel you can handle more, go ahead and invite them. If having a lot of people around gives you the jitters, keep your parties small.

To ease stress, try to anticipate who's coming. When someone replies to your invitation, ask if he or she is bringing a guest and, if so, whom. If you are hosting a party for someone else, familiarize yourself with the guest list. If an unexpected guest shows up, don't fret—set another place at the table. No one will remember a slightly crowded table, but all will note how graciously you handled an awkward situation. Some may not even notice a problem. If you do not have enough food or drink, quietly forfeit some or all of your own. You can always sneak away to the kitchen for a snack or eat something later, while cleaning up.

A great mix *of guests, enjoying themselves, is your main goal. Strive for a lively combination of personalities and interests.*

MIXING IT UP

For many of us, a party provides one of the few opportunities we get to meet people beyond our work, neighborhood, or children's circles. Take risks. Maybe your friends won't all like each other. If they don't, they won't have to see each other again. But they'll all have a chance to forge new relationships—and you'll have a chance to see many friends at once.

Try for balance among your guests. At the table, seat extroverts next to shy people, women next to men, twentysomethings next to grandmothers. Encourage intermingling, but if like types end up pairing off or congregating—and they often tend to—don't despair. Everyone is still having a good time.

An exception to mixing is the case of the single-interest group. Perhaps you're an avid reader, gourmet cook, or wine collector. Then enjoy having like-minded friends over to get to know one another and exchange ideas and the latest news.

Birthday parties, holiday gatherings, backyard barbecues, and beach picnics are enhanced by the presence of children. Start these occasions early, have plenty of the snacks kids like on hand, and plan lots of games and sports. When children are not welcome, state this tactfully in your invitation. If a parent does push the point, explain gently but firmly that the event is for grown-ups only, that you've made no arrangements for children, and that you wouldn't want any of your other guests to feel uncomfortable.

STICKY SITUATIONS

Invariably an occasion will arise when you have left someone out, whether by intention or accident. In rare circumstances, uninvited guests will catch wind of your party and will call you to ask why they were not invited, or they will ask to be invited. It is a sticky situation that should be handled tactfully. You have two choices. One is to explain that you had to limit the size of your party and, as difficult as it was, there were some friends that you were not able to invite. Be diplomatic and gracious. If you find that too direct, extend that person an invitation. Explain that it was an oversight, and you would be happy to include them. Sometimes it is easier to make an extra place at the table than it is to explain why someone wasn't invited.

Entertaining
With a Theme

---✳---

THE OCCASION—COUSIN FRED'S BIRTHDAY, YOUR BEST-FRIEND AMANDA'S PROMOTION, ARBOR DAY—IS THE REASON FOR ENTERTAINING. ASSIGNING A THEME TO THE OCCASION SETS THE TONE AND THE MOOD.

Themed parties are not for everyone, or for every occasion, but they can be a lot of fun. Don't shy away from the idea because you think a theme has to be elaborate, expensive, or time-consuming. It doesn't. Approach it playfully, and you may wind up with a party that your guests will enjoy and talk about for years to come.

Announce your theme in the invitation and say clearly to what extent you want guests to participate. (Those who feel less than enthusiastic about participating in such an event can opt out early.)

An idea for a theme can begin with the occasion. Perhaps you'd like to throw a birthday dinner for a Francophile friend. Call it "An Evening in Provence." Set the table with colorful pottery and bouquets of sunflowers, serve Provençal food and wine, and voilà—you have the next best thing to being in the French countryside.

A golden anniversary becomes a sparkling event with a little spray paint and ingenuity. Paint plastic fruit gold and pile it in bowls. Buy plastic foam rings and spray them gold, then hang them on

Involve guests by asking them to dress
in accordance with your theme.

PROPS FOR POOLSIDE PARTIES

A POOL PARTY TO CELEBRATE summer is a perfect opportunity to add festive—and practical—decorations. To make the most impact, incorporate the theme into as many elements as possible—from invitations to party favors. A shopping trip through a dime store or party-goods store will yield everything you need.

Create a playful *centerpiece with useful items such as sunscreen, disposable cameras, children's flippers, and games—all stuffed into a giant straw summer hat.*

Send party favors home *with your guests by passing out inexpensive toys and sunglasses shaped like stars.*

Write invitations *on fun items you can mail, such as kids' inflatable swimming aids.*

Fill a children's wading pool *with ice to chill soft drinks and beer.*

the front door. Ask guests to bring gifts that are gold in color and wrapped in gold paper and ribbon to continue the theme.

INVOLVING GUESTS

Involve your guests by assigning them tasks. Ask them to dress the part or contribute a food or decoration that fits the theme. Have you always wanted to host a barbecue? Make it a Western party. Stage a cookout complete with Texas barbecue, bandanna napkins, and a musician playing cowboy songs. Or make it a spaghetti Western party with a Sergio Leone video in the background. Serve pasta with red sauce, bread sticks, and Chianti on a colorful checkered tablecloth.

If you're hosting an engagement party, turn it into an elegant dinner dance. Encourage formal evening attire (which guests can buy at thrift shops), play big-band music, and, for inspiration, show videos of Fred Astaire and Ginger Rogers.

Do What Worked

Originality counts only sometimes. If you've been to a party that had a theme you really enjoyed, like a "dead celebrities" Halloween bash, or a "come as you were" party, create a similar party for your friends.

Awards event, they can cast their vote while having fun by dressing like their favorite Oscar contender—in the role for which the star is nominated.

Use the first day of the work week as an excuse for a Blue Monday party. Ask guests to dress in blue and bring a blues CD. Serve blue drinks and food.

Get your inspiration for activities from the setting. Host a desert-island theme party at the beach or hold a sand-castle

A theme is optional. Pick a theme for your party only when you think it will be fun, then embrace your choice with passion and enthusiasm.

Rent martini and highball glasses and serve classic cocktails, or invite guests to bring their own spirits. You can provide all the trimmings such as olives, wedges of fruit, and maraschino cherries.

Mark the opening day of baseball season by having your guests wear their favorite team's baseball hat, then serve— what else?—beer, peanuts, and hot dogs.

For a Grammy Awards–watching party, guests can bring an instrument or their favorite single; for an Academy

building contest. Stage a mountain-bike rally at a park in the hills and enjoy a little competition among friends before savoring a hearty picnic. For a children's birthday party that also includes parents, ask each adult to bring a beloved entrée from his or her own childhood.

Remember, a party theme is optional, an added extra. Pick a theme for your party only when you think it will be fun; then embrace your choice with passion and enthusiasm and your guests will too.

GETTING under
Way

—✳—

1 Make a schedule and set aside at least a half hour each day for **party preparation.** **2** List your **tasks** and attack them with confidence and a spirit of fun. **3** Provide guests with six weeks' **notice** for a formal event or a party that will take place during the holidays. **4** **Energize** invitations by including novel elements like confetti or a photo. **5** If you **invite guests** by phone, keep a list of those you called, those you spoke with, and those you're still waiting to hear from. **6** **Make a list** of what you have and what you need to borrow, rent, or buy. **7** Browse through a **restaurant-supply** store for everything from baking pans to aprons. Professional-quality items are often sold there at discount prices. **8** **Anticipate** glitches—such as guests arriving early—and think of solutions in advance. **9** To maintain good relations with your neighbors, **invite** them to your party even if you know they won't come. Keep the noise level tolerable. ●

MOVING
PLANS FORWARD

TRANSLATING IDEAS INTO REALITY

* — ✳ — *

Congratulations—you're giving a party! Now for the most challenging part: How can you get everything done on time? The answer is to think things through, envisioning every stage of your event from start to finish.

Move forward by scheduling manageable tasks you can perform in the course of your daily routine. If you're a born procrastinator, do the jobs you enjoy and farm out the rest. Take a vacation day from work if you must. It will be worth it to have those extra hours to prepare.

Inviting people to a party is like describing a movie: You want to entice them to the theater, but avoid giving away so much that you spoil the ending. Your invitations should convey excitement without spelling everything out.

The most important thing is to have fun. Entertaining involves careful planning to ensure that you—as well as your guests—enjoy every moment.

SCHEDULING

--- ✳ ---

WHEN IT COMES TO PLANNING ALL BUT THE MOST IMPROMPTU PARTY, A DETAILED SCHEDULE OF TASKS WILL PROVE TO BE YOUR LIFESAVER. EVEN IF YOU LOVE SURPRISES, THIS IS NOT THE TIME FOR THEM.

One hour before your guests are due to arrive is the wrong time to realize you've forgotten to order the cocktail napkins.

Try to avoid hosting a large gathering if your calendar is already packed. Allow at least one month between the time you decide to entertain and the big day itself. The earlier you begin planning, the sooner you can leap into action. You can make tasks manageable by spreading them out over the course of the weeks leading to your party. Try to stay on schedule and work ahead of time if you can.

Set aside half an hour to an hour each day for party prep. Keep a master list of tasks to be done and tackle one of them each day—more if time permits. As you accomplish each task, check it off on your list. This method allows you to get many of your major decisions and crucial tasks

Don't plan an elaborate party when your schedule is already overburdened.

PARTY-PLANNING TIMETABLE

✳

HERE'S A TASK-BY-TASK GUIDE to getting organized quickly and easily. It may seem like a lot, but remember, the work is spread out over several weeks. Take a deep breath and dive into the details.

	2–4 weeks before	3–5 days before	24 hours before	Few hours before
PLANNING				
Select the site and date; send invitations	●			
Assign tasks to helpers; hire any professionals	●			
Plan food and bar menus; decide on a theme (if any)	●			
Call to confirm arrival times for professional services			●	
SHOPPING				
Purchase bar supplies	●			
Buy equipment, supplies, and nonperishable foods	●			
Shop for perishable groceries			●	
Pick up cakes, flowers, and prepared dishes			●	
Buy last-minute provisions such as ice				●
COOKING				
Finalize the menu	●			
Prepare foods you will freeze	●			
Prepare foods you will refrigerate			●	
Cut up ingredients for salads and stir-fries			●	
Thaw frozen dishes			●	
Prepare last-minute dishes				●
SETUP				
Clean china and crystal		●		
Assemble music tapes; set up music equipment		●		
Give bathrooms and guest rooms a thorough cleaning			●	
Pick up or await rentals			●	
Arrange the flowers				●
Clean the kitchen			●	
Set up the bar and set the table			●	
Decorate according to theme (if any)			●	
Arrange buffets				●
Fill serving dishes, wrap with plastic, set out				●
Ice down the champagne				●

Don't Overdo It

Avoid overscheduling the days close to your party. Instead, space out your to-do list over less busy times. Once you've committed to having a party, avoid scheduling other social engagements that will conflict with making yours a success.

out of the way well in advance and leaves more time for creative extra touches and last-minute brainstorms.

STARTING EARLY

One month before the party, tackle these tasks: Inspect and reserve a party location. Contact caterers or other professional services to request proposals or to reserve the date. Plan food and bar menus and make a shopping list for each. Buy or make the invitations and begin writing them.

(Break up the job by dividing your guest list into sevenths and addressing one block of invitations each day for a week.) If your party has a theme, flesh it out. Jot down ideas for tying your theme to decorations, costumes, games, and snacks. Keep these notes handy as you shop for supplies and services. Make arrangements to obtain the supplies you'll need to rent as soon as possible. If you have a regular housecleaner, instruct the person about special services you'll need the week before the party, such as dusting platters, cleaning wineglasses, or polishing silverware. Assign other tasks to willing participants.

By the time the big day arrives, you'll be ready for the finishing touches. If you have help, rally everyone early. Go over what still needs to be done and what you expect of each helper during the course of the party. Then take off your apron and have a wonderful time.

By candle-lighting time, *all should be in place for your guests. Take a moment to relax and admire your handiwork.*

CREATIVE INVITATIONS

※

YOUR INVITATION IS THE FIRST IMPRESSION YOUR PARTY MAKES ON THOSE YOU'VE INVITED. A GOOD INVITATION HEIGHTENS CURIOSITY, WHETS THE APPETITE FOR FUN, AND SAYS THAT THIS IS AN EVENT NOT TO BE MISSED.

Create an invitation that reflects the occasion for your party, its theme, or the season of the year. The tone, like the event itself, is up to you. You can make it humorous, touching, dramatic, or festive.

Regardless of the style of your party, the timing of your invitations is important. Provide at least four weeks' advance notice for a formal event or for a party that will take place during the holidays (when party calendars fill up quickly). During less busy times of the year, two to three weeks should give all of your guests plenty of time to plan ahead. If you're staging an impromptu gathering, naturally call your friends whenever the idea strikes (the sooner, of course, the better).

You don't have to send an invitation if a phone call will do the trick. But if you have time or the inclination, a handcrafted invitation adds a special touch to your party. It will seem as if the fun has

---

SIMPLE SOLUTIONS

SAVE-THE-DATE ANNOUNCEMENTS

YOU'RE PLANNING A PARTY during the holidays or another time when calendars fill up fast. So far, all you know about your party is the date, so you can't send invitations. The solution: Save-the-date announcements. They let your friends decide now whether they can attend, and you get a preliminary head count.

Simple Buy attractive preprinted cards from a stationery store and fill in the date of the party. Or use a computer program to design cards that you can print out and mail.

Simpler Call or e-mail the people you'd like to see at your party, tell them your plans, and explain that you'll follow up with a detailed invitation just as soon as you've finalized the arrangements.

Simplest For dramatic appeal, tear off a calendar page, circle the date, and add a little note about your party. Fax it to potential guests or make photocopies and mail them.

PLANNING A FORMAL LUNCHEON, OR A BLOWOUT EXTRAVAGANZA? ENCLOSE OR GLUE ON OBJECTS THAT COMMUNICATE YOUR THEME WITH FLAIR.

A garden-party theme

Enclose objects that are related to the site or theme of your party. If you're having a garden party, glue purchased dried flowers onto handwritten invitations or preprinted cards. Address the envelopes, enclose the invitations, and drop in additional pressed flowers. Decorate the envelopes with a rubber stamp or simple sketches.

A festive celebration

For a gala holiday or black-tie party, write your invitations on festive, star-studded cards. These are available at stationery stores and even some copy shops. Inscribe your invitation and place in a brightly colored envelope. Add star-shaped confetti that will spill out when opened.

started even before the day arrives. Playing graphic designer is a cinch—even if you think you don't have an artistic cell in your brain. Print your invitations on squares of lightweight, colored paper, then fold each sheet into an origami shape—or just fold into triangles or squares. Slide your party invitations into contrasting, brightly colored envelopes and mail. You can top them off with a fun stamp.

If you want to send something a little more sophisticated, ask an artistic friend to draw an appropriate picture for you, then photocopy it onto heavyweight paper. Or round up a photograph (preferably one of an honored guest or capturing the event's

For a spur-of-the-moment get-together, or if you need to contact a big crowd—especially if your event is business related—it's OK to fax or e-mail your invitations.

theme) and have it printed onto the invitations at your neighborhood copy shop. Black-and-white photos copy best.

Use the invitation to introduce your theme. For a costume party, buy colorful, inexpensive paper masks and write your invitations on the backs. For a Mardi Gras party, write the details on oversize "price tags" and tie them to strings of brightly colored beads. For a backyard luau or other tropical-theme event, tie the same kind of tag to a pair of children's inexpensive sunglasses. For a holiday party, spell out your party plans on a ball ornament and wrap it in a colorful gift box.

PERSONAL TOUCHES

Using a computer, you can create invitations that are as simple as black type on white paper or as elaborate as colored ink on a textured background. Most word-processing programs include some type of graphics. Choose images, from clowns to Santa Clauses, and arrange them on the page. You can print your design on your choice of colored and textured papers, or use a color printer at a copy center. These copy centers, and most stationery stores, also sell blank invitation cards you can run through printers and copiers.

If your tight schedule or the formality of the occasion calls for printed invitations, go to a stationery store and buy cards you can fill in, or look through an order book. You can still impart your own personality on a premade card. Buy a calligraphy pen and address the envelopes. Or round up some colored markers and ask your kids to decorate the envelopes. Use colorful stamps for postage.

ELECTRONIC ETIQUETTE

In this electronic day and age, there's no reason not to take advantage of modern technologies. For a spur-of-the-moment get-together, or if you need to contact a large crowd—especially if your event is business-related—it's OK to fax or e-mail your invitations. For some of your guests, this may be the most effective means of reaching them in time. Just bear in mind that if you use the fax machine, people other than the targeted recipient (such as their coworkers) will probably see your message, whether you intend it or not.

Computers *can certainly make life simpler; use them to generate guest lists, design invitations, and track acceptances.*

Phoning guests remains a tried-and-true option. Just be sure to keep a list showing whom you called; whom you reached; and whose voice mail, administrative assistant, spouse, or children fielded the calls. If you leave a message, request that your call be returned. If a week passes and you haven't heard, try calling again.

Regrets Only

To save time and keep it simple, ask guests to respond to your invitation only if they *cannot* attend the party. This lets you keep a head count without being overwhelmed by phone calls.

If you have the time, nothing conveys your message as thoughtfully as a handwritten invitation. It is possible to produce these gems without disrupting your life by parceling them out over the course of a week. Set aside some time each day to write and address invitations; say, for half an hour during your morning coffee, as you relax with a glass of wine before dinner, or just before you get ready for bed.

Track the responses to your written invitations by listing each guest, his or her escort, and any children who may attend. Check off names as you extend the invitations, then circle them (or cross them off) as the responses come in.

DETAILS, DETAILS

Even the cleverest invitation is of little use if it leaves out essential information.

Write out the date (including the day of the week), the starting time, and the ending time if there is one. Specify the attire in detail (instead of "Casual," say "Shorts and T-shirt") so your guests won't have any question as to the mode of dress. If temperatures may be colder or warmer than expected, warn them to dress accordingly.

If you're entertaining people who have never been to your home, make sure you include detailed directions that show the easiest route to your house. If parking is at a premium in your neighborhood and visitors tend to block driveways, give some hints on where to find parking and suggest that guests carpool.

If your house is hard to find or if the party site is remote, mark the route on the day of the party by posting bright signs or balloons along the way.

A simple, handcrafted invitation makes guests feel as though the fun has already started.

TAKING INVENTORY

---✳---

NO MATTER HOW LARGE OR SMALL YOUR PARTY, THE PREPARATIONS WILL FLOW MUCH MORE SMOOTHLY IF YOU DECIDE EARLY ON WHAT YOU ALREADY HAVE AND WHAT ITEMS YOU WILL NEED TO BUY, BORROW, OR RENT.

To simplify this process, draw up a list. Visualize the event from beginning to end and jot down each element as it comes to mind. Note the location, the occasion and theme, and the number of guests. List the food and beverages you plan to serve and in what style. Ask yourself: Will this be a formal sit-down dinner? A full-course buffet with a central serving area? A simple cocktail party with snacks arranged around the living room? What time of year is it? What's the likelihood of rain or snow or wide fluctuations in temperature? Will any of your guests need special accommodations, such as ramps or doorways with wide clearances for wheelchairs?

NARROWING DOWN

Begin with the obvious. Take inventory of your chairs, benches, stools, and other seating options. Can they accommodate your group? If not, look for alternatives, such as large pillows you can arrange on the floor. Will your dinner guests fit comfortably around your table? If not, make it bigger in a flash by extending it with a piece of plywood, or haul in the picnic table from the deck. Consider a separate table for the kids. If all this expanded furniture leaves the dining room cramped, move your party to another part of the house—or outside if the weather is warm.

Make sure your cooking facilities are up to the task. If you're hosting a barbecue, for instance, make sure your grill can handle the amount of food you need to cook, and that it's set up for efficient use. Would the process be easier if you had a small table for the serving dishes and barbecue tools? Is the grill reliable enough for a special event? What about that wobbly leg you never got around to fixing?

For an outdoor summer event, you'll need something to shade both people and food from the hot sun. And if darkness will fall during the course of the party, you'll need lights. Candles, hurricane lamps, or tiki torches all fit the bill smartly. So do

Check Cords and Gas Lines

While you're going through your inventory, examine seldom-used electrical items, such as fans, blenders, or outdoor lights. Check for any frayed cords and turn the items on and off a few times to make sure they work. Also look over your outdoor barbecue for loose gas lines.

Double-Duty Items

As you work, look for objects that can be used for double duty so you don't have to buy, borrow, or rent. Bring garden furniture inside when you need extra chairs or tables. Cover a baking sheet or shallow pan with decorative napkins and use it as a tray for serving or clearing. Check that your shower curtain rod is securely attached, then use it for raincoats and other lightweight items.

small electric lamps; just make sure you have enough insulated extension cords and electrical outlets to accommodate them.

You'll need a container for cold drinks and ice, and maybe an extra garbage can, a recycling bin, or heavy-duty trash bags to hold discarded utensils and plates.

AROUND YOUR HOUSE

You may be able to cook for any size crowd in your well-equipped kitchen, but your serving gear might be inadequate. Do you have enough platters, bowls, serving trays, and spoons? Can your coffeepot make at least one cup for every guest? If not, do you have large thermos flasks to hold coffee while more is brewing?

As you take inventory, assess the condition of serving pieces. Could the silver coffee service stand a thorough polishing? Are there cracks in your ironstone platter?

Also make sure that tables and chairs are in fine shape, clean, and sturdy enough to support the weight they'll bear.

Explore your hall closet. Can it hold all your guests' coats? (For a winter party, you'll need a lot of room.) When entertaining in cold or rainy weather, you may need extra coat hangers, a coatrack, an umbrella bucket, or a tub for wet boots.

Then take a look outside. Do you have enough space in the front of your house or driveway to park cars? Will you need to enlist a valet service or ask neighbors for additional parking space? Does your porch light shine brightly enough to guide guests to the front door, or could you use candles or tiki torches to add more light? Is your house number well-lit and clearly visible—even at night?

When you take inventory, don't worry if you don't have everything you need; you probably won't, and that's fine. Listing the

As you take inventory, assess the condition of serving equipment. Also make sure tables and chairs are in fine shape, clean, and able to support the weight they'll bear.

equipment you need to buy or change at this stage is critical because it is still early enough to make changes. The plans should not be set in stone yet.

Assessing what you have on hand can help you evaluate how much effort your party will require. Concentrate on how to accomplish your party goals, and don't overlook the small details.

OUTDOOR PARTY WARE

✳

WHETHER YOU'RE HOSTING a sit-down dinner in your garden or a tailgate party in a parking lot, festive, inexpensive items can transform the decor. Safety is an issue outdoors, especially in summer when people go barefoot, so use plastic or metal dishes and glassware. Light the way with votive candles.

Use colorful, disposable plates, *cups, and utensils to save on cleanup time. A child's beach pail is a playful yet functional holder.*

Create unusual place "cards" *by writing guests' names on smooth stones or large leaves.*

Light citronella candles *to help keep pests away. Place candles in pretty holders such as shells or clay pots.*

Collect stylish lanterns *like these to add ambient lighting. Alternatively, stake out the party area with tiki torches or put up festive strings of lights.*

GATHER AND SHOP

*

W E ALL LIKE TO BE EQUIPPED TO ENTERTAIN GRACIOUSLY OR THROW A SPUR-OF-THE-MOMENT GET-TOGETHER. BUT EVEN IF THE PARTY BUG HAS BITTEN YOU HARD, THERE'S NO NEED TO BUY EVERYTHING IN SIGHT.

For one thing, you'd probably deplete your savings; for another, you might have to rent a locker to hold everything. Step back. Buy pieces you know you'll use again, and rent or borrow the rest.

Don't be afraid to ask friends, family, and neighbors if you can borrow supplies that you don't have on hand: an ice bucket, folding chairs, a punch bowl and cups, large serving platters, or extra glassware and dishes are among the items you don't necessarily want to buy.

You might ask friends who also enjoy entertaining to consider a joint investment in serving equipment or party supplies as a way to bring down the price.

Large outdoor events *usually call for rented tables and chairs—even linens. Centerpieces can be as simple as seasonal blooms.*

If you're hosting a large crowd, use a party-rental service. For a reasonable fee, these firms can supply virtually everything you need, from china, flatware, and coffee urns to barbecue grills, table linens, and crystal beverage pitchers.

Rental businesses are especially handy for obtaining things you really don't need to own, like a portable dance floor or a set of heaters big enough to warm your whole backyard. Many companies will set up and break down anything you rent, and launder linens as part of the rental (or for an additional fee).

Place your order as far in advance as possible, and if you're unsure about final numbers, reserve more of everything than you think you'll need. You can always cut back on quantities at the last minute, but

you may not be able to increase your order, especially during peak seasons. Be sure to keep a list of everything you ask for, down to the last swizzle stick. Read the rental agreement carefully before you sign. Most companies require a deposit when you place your order, and you may forfeit it if your plans change and you don't cancel within a specified time.

Find out whether you are responsible for broken, lost, or stolen supplies and whether you must rinse plates, glasses, and flatware before returning them. Frequently there's a fee if you don't.

If you have the time and your order is small, pick it up yourself. That way you can make sure everything is exactly what you asked for and in top condition. For large orders or when time is short, opt for the company's delivery and pickup service. Have the company deliver the day before the event or early that morning. Then, as you unpack, count each item and check it against your list and the company's packing slip. If you find any discrepancies, call immediately and reconcile differences. As you pack the shipment for return, check for breakage and count everything to make sure that nothing is missing.

OFF THE BEATEN PATH

Often the best party gear lurks in places other than your local stores. One terrific place to shop for everything from baking pans to aprons is restaurant-supply stores. There you'll find specialized, professional-quality equipment, frequently at discount prices. You may want to invest in things you'll use long after the party's over. Other

Become a Thrift Shopper

A trip to a secondhand store, thrift shop, or garage sale can be a host's nirvana. Here you might find china, silver, and glassware treasures that can embellish your household long after your guests have departed. You can also find things you'll use only at party time—serving trays, coffeemakers, ashtrays— at prices too good to pass up.

places you should consider: antique markets, for treasures that are as decorative as they are functional, and often at prices well below those in housewares stores; Asian shops, for woks and rice cookers; and Hispanic markets, for piñatas, festive Mexican pottery, or sturdy glasses.

SHOPPING EFFICIENTLY

How many times have you gone inside a store and come out with none of the things you needed and bags full of things you didn't? Have you ever spent hours driving from place to place in search of that elusive, essential object? Do you wonder how some people can simply go out, find what they want, and come home again?

You can too. First, make a list of everything you need to obtain, from frying pans to candle holders, and note things you can borrow. Then divide the rest of the list— the stuff you need to buy—into categories such as snacks, decorations, and cooking gear. Next to each item, jot down the name of a store in your area that carries it. If your list includes the names of more than three stores, reconsider your shopping list. You might not need to buy some of those items after all. Most likely you'll come across more-than-suitable substitutes during your three-store shopping excursion.

regular commute to and from work, or on other routes you travel frequently. Make a mental driving trip to each store to figure out the easiest route.

Keep an eye out for sales, discounts, off-season bargains, and deals on bulk goods. Throughout the year, stock up on things you'll use at party time: cocktail napkins, candles, stemware. Set aside part

If you entertain frequently, keep a list of things you'd like to own. You can buy a piece at a time if you can't afford a whole set.

For peak efficiency, shop in your neighborhood and at stores where you know the stock and the layout. Cultivate friendly relationships with shop staff and grocery clerks. They can provide invaluable assistance when you're in a hurry or need help locating something out of the ordinary. Visit the shops and stores that are on your

of a closet or cabinet for party gear, or find a trunk and dedicate it to the cause.

Mail-order and, in recent years, online catalogs offer untold riches for the creative party giver. You can browse for everything from specialized cookware to personalized welcome mats without leaving the comfort of your home.

FUTURE INVESTMENTS

Consider every purchase an investment in future entertaining and in your home. When you find something you love, and you think you can use it over and over, buy it if you possibly can. The handblown votive holder you fell in love with in the glassmaker's studio will take center stage on the mantel for years to come, evoking fond memories every time you look at it. Even if you have to splurge, the expense will be well worth it in the long run.

If you entertain frequently, keep a list of items you'd like to own. Take a minute to recall, over the course of a year, every time you've rented or borrowed something or used a substitute that didn't quite make

Buy in Bulk

With bulk packages appearing everyplace from warehouse stores to supermarkets, it's easier than ever to stock up on dry goods and nonperishable party foods. Buy plastic cups and utensils, paper plates and napkins, individually sealed packages of crackers and chips, and cans of beans and sauces. That way you'll always have party fixings whenever you need them, and you'll save money too.

If you entertain often, it pays to stock up
when nonperishable party goods go on sale.

the grade. At first glance, a large-capacity blender might seem a frivolous purchase. But if you give more than a few parties a year and rent a blender every time, the purchase will pay for itself before you know it—especially if you find one on sale or at a discount restaurant-supply store.

Your wish list can also help you amass a dream collection—perhaps a collection of crystal champagne flutes or an impressive array of Italian ceramic plates. Maybe you can't afford whole sets right now, but if you want them enough to put them on your list, consider building sets by buying a piece or two at a time, perhaps as a treat to yourself on special occasions.

Remember, you don't have to buy or rent if you can borrow from others. Just be gracious about it—be punctual in your return and make sure that whatever you've

borrowed goes back in the same shape or better. Thank those you've borrowed from, and offer to return the favor. When your needs call for larger or more elaborate items, rent the big stuff and accumulate the rest of the materials over time. Buy only what you truly want to own and only if you can justify the expense.

Call Ahead

Need something out of the ordinary? Before you jump in the car, check the Yellow Pages. Even if you're certain a store has what you want, make sure the item is in stock.

DON'T PANIC—
TROUBLESHOOT!

✳

PICTURE THIS IF YOU WILL: IN HALF AN HOUR, 200 GUESTS WILL DESCEND ON YOU FOR A LUNCHEON RECEPTION YOU'VE BEEN PLANNING FOR MONTHS, AND THE RENTAL COMPANY HASN'T DELIVERED YOUR TABLES TO THE SITE.

Or this: You walk into the kitchen just in time to see your dog polishing off an expensive chateaubriand. Or: Your cocktail party is in full swing when the power goes out. These things do happen. What makes the difference between a catastrophe and a mishap you'll laugh about later is one simple thing: disaster planning.

The best way to resolve a problem is to anticipate and avoid it. Picture your party at every step. Imagine the worst that could possibly happen—within reason—then decide in advance how to cope. For example, what if guests should arrive early while you're still making the salad or setting the table? Be ready by finishing the last detail a half hour before you expect the first arrival. If that's impossible, designate a friend, your spouse, or another relative to serve as official greeter. While you're busy, the designated greeter can take coats, offer drinks and hors d'oeuvres to your guests, and make them feel welcome.

BEING PREPARED

Confirm delivery times, pickups, and other services at least a day in advance. And cultivate backup resources. That way, if your caterer vanishes, you can call a restaurant or take-out shop—and know they'll show up. Get to know neighborhood teenagers so if the babysitter doesn't show, you'll

Don't overreact when an accident happens. Just clean it up
and get on with the party. Your cool will be admired.

have an alternate. Turn a bedroom into a playground. Keep lots of toys and games on hand for children of all ages.

Keep a small first-aid kit handy. Post emergency numbers next to the phone so if there's a medical crisis, anyone can come to the rescue. A stash of candles, oil lamps, and flashlights can turn a power outage into a romantic adventure. Nothing can do that for a plumbing emergency, but a nearby plunger can avert disaster. And always, always have a rainy-day alternative for any outdoor event.

If your soufflé falls, your barbecued chicken turns to charcoal, or your soup never thickens, stay calm. Keep a straight face. Pretend that's the way you intended it and no one will be the wiser. People will be more likely to believe you if you say it with enough conviction.

To maintain good relations with your neighbors, invite them to the party even if you know they won't come. And whether they join you or not, be considerate: One person's music is another's noise. Turn music down or off late at night. Ask your local law enforcement agency about noise ordinances and parking regulations.

UNFORESEEN EVENTS

A party isn't a party unless something gets broken. If you don't want to sacrifice a cherished item to Bacchus, the party god, keep it away from the action. But if the caterer smashes your favorite Waterford bowl or a guest spills glögg on your white sofa, stay calm. Clean up the mess and get on with the party. Objects can be replaced; friends can't. Your cool will be admired.

Keeping Mud at Bay

An unexpected rainy day with an army of guests in your home doesn't have to spell muddy disaster for your floors. Ask guests to remove their shoes at the front door. Have a basketful of clean, warm socks or slippers of varying sizes waiting for anyone who needs them. Besides keeping mud out of your house, this simple solution will have your guests buffing your floors as they mingle!

What about the guest who winds up with fettuccine Alfredo all over his shirt? Take him aside, give him a roll of paper towels, and show him to the bathroom.

Most party givers face one hurdle that could result in true disaster: how to handle the guest who's drunk too much. One way to avoid the situation is to set a cutoff time for the bar; after that, pour only non-alcoholic drinks. Otherwise, if someone has overindulged, put the guest up in your spare room, call a cab, or ask a guest you trust to drive the person home.

Small setbacks occur, but the biggest disasters rarely happen. If you are ready for small mishaps you will be all the more relieved when they don't happen. And if worse comes to worst, keep your sense of humor. Even the most trying moments are brighter if you can laugh them off.

GET OTHERS to
Pitch In

—✳—

1 Use **friends** and loved ones as a sounding board to help you plan. **2** Have your **bartender** focus on one special kind of drink—martinis, microbrews, fresh-fruit smoothies whipped up in a blender—to cut down on complexity. **3** Take advantage of your **caterer's** specific areas of expertise, such as a knack for a particular cuisine. **4** Hire a **decorator,** even if only as a consultant, with whom you can bounce around ideas. **5** Ask a **florist** to decorate with centerpieces made of flowers, candles, or seasonal foliage. **6** Prepare for an outdoor party by having a **gardener** mow the lawn and remove sickly plants. **7** Never underestimate the value of **kitchen help**—hire a teenager to wash the dishes. **8** If parking is difficult at your site, hire a **valet. 9** Find a professional **entertainer** to amuse your guests, or ask talented friends to show off their skills. **10** If time is tight, use a professional **party planner** to handle logistics and execution. ●

ASKING
FOR HELP

GETTING OTHERS TO HELP
EASE YOUR LOAD

* —— * —— *

The larger and more elaborate a party is, the more work it takes. But don't let that fact deter you. Three simple rules apply for entertaining on a grand scale: delegate, delegate, delegate. Having enough help can spell the difference between a gathering that comes off like a dream and an experience that leaves you swearing you'll never go through that again.

You might find it difficult to ask for help. If you do it gracefully (and don't take advantage of people), your family, friends, and coworkers probably won't mind. People love sharing their talents and resources, and you can reciprocate the next time they entertain. But do call in professionals for large parties when you want to make an impression and still spend time with your guests. If your budget won't allow their full services, have the pros do just the chores you don't enjoy, delegate others, and do the rest of the tasks yourself.

LET EVERYONE HELP

---✳---

LIKE MANY GOOD THINGS IN LIFE, GREAT HELP LIES CLOSE TO HOME. CALL ON THE PEOPLE WHO KNOW YOU BEST: YOUR SIBLINGS, YOUR PARENTS, YOUR BEST FRIEND. YOU KNOW YOU CAN TRUST THEM TO PROVIDE ASSISTANCE.

After all, they've backed you through everything from your algebra finals to changing jobs, right? Who else can you count on to watch the kids, make a killer potato salad, or pick up the things you've forgotten?

As the countdown proceeds, even the most experienced hosts feel a little nervous. Having people you trust around will calm your jitters and lighten your mood, and loved ones provide a good sounding board for ideas during the planning stages.

Your ace in the hole could be a friend who entertains often. She'll be flattered

Get your kids *and their friends involved with decorations. Throwing a birthday party is more fun if you make it a family affair.*

that you asked her to share her knowledge; you'll benefit by hearing educated opinions about everything from party planners to cocktail napkins. Frequent party givers can also simplify your search for supplies. They'll have decorations, serving platters, games, extra chairs, and other items you can borrow. They'll probably enjoy making a contribution to the occasion, and you'll be spared some time- and money-consuming shopping trips.

CREATIVE SOLUTIONS

Face it, nobody's a whiz at everything. But you can come off looking like one simply by calling for help. Got a tin ear? Ask a musical friend to audition the piano player or tape two hours of uninterrupted music. If you'll be busy preparing food, ask Uncle Charlie to tend the grill. Got a friend who takes great photos? Turn your camera over to her. Later, when you send copies to your guests, they're bound to be touched by your thoughtfulness and unlikely to focus on who took the shots.

When a guest offers to bring something, don't be shy; say, "Thank you, yes, please!" People like to feel they've made a contribution to the success of an event— and it's a rare gathering that can't absorb an extra bag of ice or a bottle of wine. Accepting an offer of food or drink makes life easier for you: it adds to your inventory and helps you offer your guests a more diverse assortment of dishes.

Once you're ready to receive guests, remember that the first impression is the most lasting. You can make a great one, even while you're darting around doing the inevitable last-minute jobs, simply by asking someone to help you greet guests. Early arrivals will feel right at home when your mother, child, spouse, or friend takes them in tow, hands them something to drink, and ushers them into the action.

If time is short and your energy level is low, you can still pull off a stylish party by making it a potluck. Do it the classic way, by assigning each guest a dish to bring, or use the concept more creatively, with, say, a French or Caribbean theme.

Now that you know whom to ask for help, keep to these ground rules. Don't ask people—no matter how closely related—to spend money or large amounts of time on your project. And always offer something in return. If your brother fixes that broken table leaf, have his car washed for him. If your neighbor lends you a truckload of chairs, offer to babysit the kids one night. If your spouse skips a tennis game to help you prepare for a baby shower, give him or her a surprise present, a card with a note, breakfast in bed, or tickets to a favorite movie or game.

AFTER GUESTS ARRIVE

Serving the meal can be one of the most overwhelming chores of entertaining. Getting everything on the table while it's hot, filling glasses, and conversing with

Give the Kids Jobs

Keep kids out from underfoot by giving them party jobs. Even young children can help dust, pick up clutter, or arrange magazines. Other children like to mingle, so you can have them greet guests and take coats. Put them to work passing hors d'oeuvres and refilling food platters. If your bash doesn't run too far past their bedtime, you can also enlist kids' help putting things away and cleaning up.

your guests all at once seems impossible. But it's not if you get help with the small details—often the easiest tasks to delegate.

Dinner preparation is full of opportunities for help. When someone offers to help, or if you feel comfortable asking for volunteers, have your guests put on aprons and assign a task to each person. Put them to work with last-minute jobs like slicing the bread, pouring wine, lighting the candles, and carrying full dishes from the kitchen to the table. You can visit with these helpers and even enjoy a cocktail while cooking your meal.

While you are in the kitchen, ask someone else to pass hors d'oeuvres or serve drinks. After all, you probably wouldn't want to sit around feeling idle if you could be helping a busy host, so why wouldn't your guests feel the same way?

WORKING WITH THE PROS

---*---

I F YOU'RE PLANNING A LARGE PARTY, YOU'LL PROBABLY NEED MORE HELP—
AND MORE EXPERTISE—THAN FRIENDS AND FAMILY CAN PROVIDE. IF YOUR
BUDGET CAN HANDLE IT, HIRE PROFESSIONALS TO EASE YOUR WORKLOAD.

Their know-how will prove invaluable if you want decorations for a special event, or a catered meal for 100. If you're holding the party at home, you may need a gardener to prepare the backyard or a valet company to park the cars.

Sometimes it certainly pays to turn your party over to someone else. You'll have much more peace of mind in the planning stages, and the satisfaction of getting exactly what you want.

PARTY PLANNERS

For a special event, if you can afford the maximum in stress-free entertaining, hire a party planner. A seasoned pro will have orchestrated

gatherings of every size in every conceivable venue, and will have developed close relationships with everyone from decorators to rental companies. If you've chosen a cruise-ship theme in a rented hall for your parents' 50th-anniversary party, and you have neither the time nor the knowledge to decorate, plan the buffet, hire entertainment, and so on, an experienced planner is exactly what you need.

Party planners guide you through the entire process, help you make the right decisions, and, best of all, do all the work.

Party-planning fees vary greatly from one company to another. Some firms start with a fee for a basic package; others base their fees on

Caterers are remarkably versatile and can
handle your specific menu requests with style.

a percentage of the gross party budget. For smaller consulting jobs, some planners charge an hourly rate that can range from reasonable to excessive. Bear in mind that a party planner's fee is strictly for planning. It does not include any of the services the planner may be securing for you, such as those of decorators, florists, or caterers. A planner's fee covers consulting time only, rather than the labor or materials. So budget accordingly to avoid any surprises.

You can find party planners in the phone book, local newspapers, and regional magazines, or call a rental company and ask for suggestions. Then interview several candidates. Ask to see their portfolios, and compare their work with your budget, your style, and the way you visualize your party. Check references and ask clients and vendors about the planners' timeliness, efficiency, and communication skills.

Once you've hired a party planner, set up a series of meetings, by phone or in person, to track progress. Be especially alert to any cost changes that crop up.

USING CATERERS

You might be a whiz in the kitchen, but that doesn't mean you have to whip up a sit-down dinner for 6 or a buffet for 60. At party time, a good caterer is a host's best friend. Don't be intimidated by the details; working with a caterer is a cinch when you follow a few simple guidelines.

Once you've selected the firm, have an initial meeting to discuss the details: your budget, the size of the guest list, the theme of the party, and, most important, the food and how you want it served. Do

SIMPLY PUT...

PAPERWORK FOR PROFESSIONALS

proposal • Also known as an estimate, this is essentially a promise from a professional to provide a range of services at a specific cost. It generally includes your event's particulars and specifies what tasks and responsibilities the service provider will assume.

contract • An agreement you enter into with the professional you've hired. Your signature is your promise to pay for the services rendered. A contract is often more specific than a proposal and includes such details as the exact menu (in the case of catering), as well as a payment schedule and liability notice.

insurance • Liability insurance that service providers carry to protect themselves (and you) if a guest becomes ill from the food, or in the event of accidents or loss. Service providers should also carry workers' compensation insurance in case one of their employees is injured while on the job and files a claim against them.

you want hors d'oeuvres passed around on trays? Box lunches served in a meadow? A formal sit-down dinner? Request any specific dishes, beverages, or serving arrangements you'd like and ask the caterer for suggestions. When in doubt, if the caterer has a solid reputation for a specialty food, order that item. By all means, sample the food and make sure it's what you want.

If your budget *allows, use caterers for special occasions that call for rented halls and lots of guests. Caterers will handle most details.*

To make your planning process simple, get all the details straight at this first meeting. Will the caterer provide tables, chairs, serving platters, and so forth, or will you? What gear will be rented and

who will take charge of it from the initial phone call to the final breakdown and return? How do you want the wait staff to dress? And what time should everyone arrive? Finally, ask the caterer to prepare a proposal based on the dishes you ordered and all the other decisions you've made during the meeting.

Next, arrange a site inspection. Give the caterer a full tour of the rooms that his or her staff will be using. If you're entertaining at home, a pro will ask to see it all and have you explain how the dishwasher works, where the garbage goes, where you keep the knives, or whether an oven knob sticks. If you're entertaining elsewhere, the caterer will meet with the manager of the hotel or hall and work out the logistics. If you have the time to meet them there, it's a good idea, but not essential.

Make meeting with caterers easy: let them be your guide. Caterers will tell you how much help they need in the kitchen and whether they or a wait captain will oversee the serving. Most likely it will be

How to Check References

Ask your final candidate for references before you decide to hire. Call at least three referrals and quiz them about product and service quality, hidden costs, and overall performance. You'll feel much more at ease if you can confirm that your preferred caterer has made other party givers happy in the past.

the latter. If it is, get to know that captain; he or she will want to know all the logistics of how you wish your party to unfold.

After you've chosen your final menu, the caterer should provide you with a contract that confirms the issues you've discussed and includes all prices and fees.

To make your planning process simple, get all the details straight at the first meeting with the caterer.

Make sure you're clear about any deposit: the amount, when it's due, and whether or not it's refundable.

Catering prices vary dramatically. A sit-down dinner for 12 can cost the same as a buffet dinner for 60. Ask your caterer to explain the price structure. The basic

fees include food and labor. You can expect charges for such things as the staff (don't be alarmed if it seems like an army; trust your caterer's judgment), transportation, rental equipment and coordination, and any additional services you ask the caterer to perform. There will also be sales tax. At your request, the caterer may hire a bartender or florist, and will tack a service fee onto the final bill.

On the day of your event, if it's at home, clear out the fridge, banish children and pets from the kitchen and work areas, discuss last-minute details, then get out of the way. If you stray into the kitchen during the preparation process, it will look as if a tornado has hit. Don't panic, though. A reputable caterer will have it shipshape before the first guest arrives.

Before the caterer leaves, pay the balance of the bill and include tips for the

Tipping

Have enough cash on hand to tip the service staff you've hired. The amount depends on the quality of the service and your budget. You can tip a flat per-person amount, or you can tip 15 to 20 percent of the total bill. Either way, give the total amount in a lump sum to the person in charge and ask him or her to disburse it.

staff if they've done a good job. If anything went awry during the party, don't settle but instead arrange to discuss final payment the next day. Ask then for compensation or an adjustment in charges.

Having a caterer who does it all, from cooking to cleanup, is a wonderful luxury. If full service is beyond your budget, you can still treat yourself: have the caterer prepare and deliver the food. You'll still have a memorable meal prepared by others but at a more affordable price.

USING DECORATORS

Decorators are magicians who work their wonders with lights, staging, and fanciful objects. If you're orchestrating a mega-event, or if only a miracle will transform your church-basement meeting room into the entertainment Taj Mahal of your dreams, call a decorator.

She or he will take your fantasy and turn it into reality—present you with a plan that's complete down to the last palm tree; then rent, beg, or borrow the necessary fixings, such as greenery, flooring, special lighting, or folding screens.

Decorating services won't come cheap, but with no effort on your part a decorator can bring your theme to life and turn an otherwise dull room into a place your guests will talk about long after they leave the party. Decorators can transform your studio apartment into a balcony in the South of France, your dining room into a trattoria in Tuscany, or your backyard into a chuck-wagon stop on the Santa Fe Trail. If large-scale transformations are out of your price range, however, you can still create enchantment by retaining a decorator as a consultant who will be a sounding board for all your ideas.

Draw up a contract that states clearly what responsibilities the decorator will assume and what costs are included.

Interior decorators are easy to find. Look in the phone book or call a party planner for referrals. Ask to see photographs of previous jobs and check references carefully to make sure candidates can deliver on time and within your allotted budget.

Then meet with your potential choices to discuss the event you have in mind and how they would execute it. Let the decorators offer their advice and opinions. Pay attention to the details of their plan, and treat this negotiation as you would any other professional service.

It's important to feel comfortable with your decorator. If you're dealing with the hottest star on your local social scene, make sure that you can call the shots. If not, hire someone else. You don't want to feel forced into a fancy budget or a theme you don't love. It's your party, after all.

Draw up a contract that states clearly what responsibilities the decorator will assume and what costs are included. For instance, if the decorator will determine the placement of flowers, ask whether the price includes the flowers and containers or only their placement.

HIRING A FLORIST

A florist can do much more than arrange flowers. A truly imaginative one can create spring in the dead of winter, transform your dining room into a tropical paradise, or turn your yard into a bountiful fall harvest. A florist can substitute for a decorator and make an impact, even if you just need a few centerpieces and an arrangement to enhance a hall or living room.

Finding a florist is as easy as picking up your phone. Call a friend or two whose arrangements you've admired—perhaps at a wedding or other formal event—and ask for names and phone numbers. Visit the shops they recommend, describe your event, and ask to see pictures of work each florist has done for similar gatherings.

Once you've made your decision, you can work with a florist in a variety of ways. (See page 112 for more information about flower arrangements.) If you know exactly what you want down to the last pink rosebud, order custom arrangements.

FLORISTS' CAPABILITIES GO FAR BEYOND ARRANGING FLOWERS IN VASES. THEY CAN ALSO WORK WITH GREENERY AND PROPS TO HELP YOU SET THE STAGE.

Creative camouflage
To camouflage a storage area or hide a busy kitchen, have your florist embellish a free-standing screen with flowers and ribbons.

Fragrant shade
Transform large, rented market umbrellas into lush tropical canopies to provide shade outdoors. Have your florist wrap fragrant climbing vines around the poles.

Space dividers
In an outdoor area, divide large expanses into several "rooms" using small potted trees. Line walkways with columns topped with trailing ivy, or urns overflowing with ferns or potted plants.

Scene setters
Does your party have a theme? If so, set the stage right at the entrance with a dramatic prop or arrangement. For a tropical-island theme, you can rent a potted palm and place coconuts around its base; for a bon-voyage party, affix picture postcards (displaying various exotic locations) to stakes of different heights and arrange them in a vase.

Have your florist create the look you want for your party. Or buy in bulk from a flower market and arrange flowers yourself.

Otherwise, describe the color scheme of the room. You and the florist will work out how many arrangements you'll need, how big you want them to be, and where they'll go. Let the florist take it from there. If you love working with flowers, have the florist buy the flowers you want and

Candles, fresh fruit, nuts, or pinecones can also add interest and sometimes cut costs, especially if they're standing in for rare or out-of-season blooms.

For no-fuss drama and to save money, order potted plants. A burst of chrysanthemums or a single, beautiful orchid can

When negotiating fees, ask whether the florist provides containers and when you'll need to return them. If they cost extra, use your own.

arrange them yourself. Always specify how long you want the arrangements to last: the staying power of cut blooms varies from scarcely a day to a week or more. If you're on a budget, buy them yourself from a flower mart.

For the sake of your pocketbook and your stress level, ask for in-season flowers. They'll always be less expensive, more plentiful, and easier to come by than their out-of-season counterparts. If you absolutely must have tulips in July or dahlias in January, ask how hard they'll be to get and what they'll cost.

look more stunning than an elaborate display of cut flowers. Your centerpieces will last long after the party's over if you use herb or ivy topiaries, or miniature roses. If you hanker for something that's not part of the florist's standard repertoire, such as a flower-covered trellis, ask to see a sample or photo before you commit to the order.

Be candid from the beginning. If you can't abide baby's breath or if stargazer lilies make your eyes water, say so. If any of your guests are allergic, or if you think they might be, say no to any heavily scented flowers, even if you love them.

And if arrangements will be placed anywhere near food or within reach of small children or inquisitive pets, tell the florist to leave out anything with poisonous leaves, seeds, or flowers. Ask for a list or get one from the poison control center if you're doing the flowers yourself. Most flowers are harmless to humans and critters alike, however, and many are edible. Ask for extra (nonpoisonous) blossoms and branches to decorate serving platters, buffet tables, and other surfaces.

When negotiating fees, ask whether the florist provides containers as part of the total price and whether you'll need to return them. If the containers cost extra, use your own vases or borrow some from friends. Finally, ask for tips on keeping the flowers fresh, and arrange for delivery as close to party time as possible so the flowers will be at their peak of perfection.

IDEAS FOR GREENERY

What do you do if you've rented a cavernous auditorium that could swallow up an entire florist shop? No problem—once you've found a plant-rental company you can get enough lush greenery and exotic blooms to turn a barren hall into a tropical isle. If you know exactly what you want, say so, confirm the price, and make delivery arrangements. If you're at a loss about where to begin, ask a few companies to come for a site visit. Tell the representatives how much you want to spend and the effect you want to create, and they'll take it from there. At least one of them should have plenty of creative ideas for you in your price range.

If your budget is too tight for the all-out treatment, make the most economical use of your florist's efforts by confining them to one or two dramatic centerpieces.

S I M P L E   S O L U T I O N S

A PARTY-READY GARDEN

TURNING A NEGLECTED YARD into a pretty space can seem like an overwhelming—and expensive—task. Enlist your family or a friend to help turn your yard into a vibrant party spot without breaking your back or your bank account.

Simple Clean up the place; mow the lawn, trim the hedges. Dig up any scruffy or dying plants and replace them with healthy new greenery, preferably flowering shrubs, from your local nursery.

Simpler Mow the lawn and trim the hedges. Remove only those ailing plants that will be within eyesight on the day of the party. Water the day before the party so the grass is dry when guests arrive.

Simplest Give your lawn and shrubs a cut. It may not sound like much, but a trim can make a huge difference. Set out new flowers and plants still in their nursery pots to fill in bare spots in the yard.

Go the rest of the way yourself by filling vases with simple bunches of a single kind of flower—purchased or plucked from your own garden—and placing them on side tables.

You say you're entertaining in your backyard and it looks about as festive as the rough at your local golf course? Not to worry: gardening help comes in many forms and all price ranges. At the bottom of the price scale there's your child, or a neighborhood teenager, who'll be happy to earn pocket money mowing the lawn or deadheading flowers. At the top there's the professional garden designer who—time and budget permitting—can create a virtual Eden in a humdrum suburban lot.

Then there's the middle-of-the-road solution: a landscape specialist who does

Flowers help make any party. *Work with blooms from your own garden or set out potted flowers from your nursery.*

heavy pruning, outdoor cleaning, and basic planting. Check the ads in your local newspaper, or look in the phone book under "Landscape Services." Better still, visit a nearby nursery—most have employees who moonlight as maintenance specialists.

Have the gardener look at your space, recommend what work needs to be done, and estimate the cost. Ask about billing. Usually the contractor will give you a verbal estimate, then present you with a bill when the work is finished.

It's often worth the expense to hire professional party services. They enable you to entertain when your calendar won't otherwise permit it. Remember, however, that even if you hire someone else to do some or all of the work, it's still *your* party. You'll need to direct such activities as generating a guest list and selecting the menu, decorations, and floral arrangements for other people to execute.

Help on the Day

---✳---

SOMETIMES YOU JUST DON'T WANT TO ASK A FRIEND OR FAMILY MEMBER TO DO CERTAIN TASKS—LIKE HELP WASH UP IN THE KITCHEN OR PARK THE CARS. EVEN AT A SMALL GATHERING, YOU MIGHT LIKE TO SPLURGE.

Hired kitchen help lets you be present at the party instead of frantic in the kitchen. Doesn't that sound worthwhile?

At a big event someone who will tend bar, clean up the dishes, serve the canapés, or park guests' cars is often worth the money so you can mingle serenely with guests, knowing that someone else is taking care of the details.

HIRING A BARTENDER

Looks easy, doesn't it—standing behind the bar, tossing in a jigger of this, a splash of that? Think again. The bar can be the busiest place at a party. You can keep it simple by serving just wine, beer, and soda. Or you can offer one type of drink and have a microbrew tasting, or a blender fresh-fruit bash. Once you move beyond that, there's a real knack to mixology. If you intend to host a large gathering and offer a full bar, you'll need a bartender who knows his or her craft.

For an informal event, you can probably get away with a knowledgeable friend or two taking charge. Put all the fixings out so they don't have to go searching for swizzle sticks or martini glasses. If you want to make the arrangement more official, hire a local college student at an hourly rate that satisfies both of you and includes setting up and breaking down the bar as well as tending it. Either way, you should invest in a good bartender's manual: It will come in handy if anyone asks for an unusual drink, and it will make a useful addition to your party-supply closet.

Once you move on to a large gathering or a business event, the caterer can probably arrange or recommend a professional bar service. It's your most reliable and stress-free option. If you need to hire one yourself, look in the phone book or call a caterer, party planner, or bartending school for suggestions. Check references to ensure that the bartender or service has the experience and work style you prefer.

Invest in a good bartender's manual. It will come in handy if anyone asks for an unusual drink, and it will make a useful addition to your party-supply closet.

Bartenders from professional services often come fully equipped with everything they need, from the bar itself to the liquor, mixers, shakers and strainers, cocktail glasses, and even the pickled onions. Ask what they'll supply. They should carry insurance against theft and damage, and a real pro will be aware of the legal penalties for serving minors or overserving anyone.

A professional bartender usually charges a per-person fee, which varies according to the types of beverages you request and hours of service. This covers all costs. You'll pay the least for a simple assortment of drinks. The next step up will be to ask for a fully stocked, standard bar; then comes a full bar stocked with premium brands. Expect extra fees if you specify French champagne instead of domestic sparkling wine; imported or microbrewery beers instead of more common brands. Always negotiate for what you want most. Request a certificate of the company's insurance when it sends you a contract, read it carefully, and keep it for your records.

KITCHEN HELP

No doubt it's possible to get through a large party without an extra pair of hands in the kitchen. But chances are you'll need help. If you would prefer not to ask guests and friends for assistance, there are other strategies you can use. Offer your baby-sitter the regular hourly rate plus dinner if he or she will help out in the kitchen. Bribe your teenager with concert tickets. If you have a regular housecleaner, ask if he or she can assist you at the usual hourly rate. Or call a culinary school and ask for a couple of students to help out.

Have your helpers arrive well before the guests are due. Conduct a thorough briefing session. Spell out the agenda for the party, and tell each person exactly what to do and at what time. Give each one a list of tasks. That way your helpers won't have to interrupt you with their questions as the evening progresses.

Pay special attention to the dishwasher (the human one, that is), as that person will handle all items that don't go into the automatic dishwasher. Provide an apron and rubber gloves. To head off flaring tempers and hurt feelings, explain how to handle anything that needs special treatment. Even if your helper is a culinary student or your best friend's child, don't assume he or she knows that your knives don't go in the dishwasher, or that you always cushion the sink with a towel before you wash the Waterford goblets.

If you're afraid of damaging the lovely Limoges platter your Aunt Mary gave you, don't use it. Or tell your helpers not to touch it, and wash it yourself later. Broken china is a fact of life at parties. So are holes burned in tablecloths, chipped stemware, mud ground into carpets, and red wine spilled on brand-new sofas. When the inevitable happens, accept it graciously, have it cleared up quickly, and get back to enjoying your party.

Give a Guided Tour

When you've hired help, explain clearly how you like your dishes stacked and your pots and pans hung. Point out switches for the disposal, dishwasher, and trash compactor. Show where you keep recycling and garbage bags. Tell how to wash special items.

VALET PARKING

If you've ever driven around and around the block in search of that elusive city parking space, you know there are times when a valet parking attendant is the most welcome sight on earth.

You could ask people to entrust their cars to your college-student nephew, or—for everyone's peace of mind—you could hire a reputable company that has fully bonded attendants with very good driving records. If something happens when an attendant is driving a guest's car, the company will be liable. When you interview companies, ask how long they have been in business, what experience they've had with private parties, and what their insurance policy covers. Request a client list, and check their references. Ask previous customers how the attendants respond in difficult situations, how quickly they retrieve cars, and whether the staff behaves in a professional manner.

If guests will be parking in a lot that's more than a couple of blocks from the party site, arrange for a shuttle service. It's

Protective Tools

Parking attendants should come fully prepared with flashlights, jackets, and any necessary signs. However, if your event site is especially dark or hard to see, you should take further precautions. Illuminate the area where the attendants will congregate; make sure they all wear bright, reflective clothing; and offer them extra flashlights.

OK to hire acquaintances and rent vans. Just make sure they have flawless driving records and sufficient liability insurance.

Most parking services charge an hourly rate per attendant. Don't skimp on the number of attendants. Expect extra fees if your party takes place outside the company's normal service area, or if a lockbox for keys is provided. Request a contract, and review it carefully for unexpected costs.

Hire a parking valet with whom you—and your guests—will be comfortable.

THAT'S ENTERTAINMENT

— ✳ —

YOU'RE SURE TO ENJOY DANCING TO A LIVE BAND; HEARING A ROOM COME ALIVE WITH HEARTY LAUGHTER; OR WATCHING A SMILE SPREAD ACROSS AN HONORED GUEST'S FACE AS A SINGER CROONS HIS FAVORITE SONG.

In these days of omnipresent television, and canned music blaring from every shop and restaurant, it's easy to forget how thrilling a live performance can be. Help your guests remember.

Your entertainers don't have to be top celebrities or even professionals if you know someone who entertains as a hobby. Make sure you match the performance with the audience, the event, and the place. Will your guests want to sit back and listen while a jazz trio holds forth in

A swing band *in a bandstand sets the scene for a memorable evening. Live music doesn't have to be expensive. Check local colleges for talented musicians.*

the garden? Or would they prefer a wild game of whodunit led by a local mystery writer or actors in character?

For an outdoor children's party, kids respond to anything that's new and fun. Hire a clown, a magician, or a troop of puppeteers to perform for the afternoon. Or give them a more hands-on experience. Find an origami artist who can show them how to fold paper animals, or a dance instructor to lead a square dance or tango.

For adults, match entertainment and theme. For a Christmas party, present carolers in full Dickensian glory. To salute friends en route to Hawaii, surprise them with a trio of hula dancers—and lessons

**Find out if any of your friends
have hidden talents you can use.**

for all after the show. Everyone enjoys hobnobbing with celebrities, and every community has Marilyn Monroe, Elvis, or John Wayne impersonators who would be happy to greet your guests.

Nothing adds sparkle to a party like a live band. Get your guests on the dance floor with a polka band, a country fiddler and square dance caller, or a Latin band pouring out hot sambas and rumbas. Or gather everybody around the piano bar for a sing-along. If you have a list of special songs you'd like the musicians to perform, give it to them ahead of time.

SCOUTING FOR TALENT

It's easy to find great entertainers, and usually the cost is not prohibitive. Call your local musicians' union or check the phone book for talent agencies. You can also inquire at nearby nightclubs. Get a price estimate and ask about details: the length of the performance, the number of breaks the musicians will take, whether you're expected to provide food and drinks.

Clarify deposit and payment requirements and ask whether any tipping is customary. Check references. Finally, make sure that the party location and its wiring system can actually accommodate the performers and all their equipment.

Whomever you choose, make sure that the type of entertainment you will be offering is appropriate for the occasion and will not offend any of your guests.

See Them in Action

Before you hire anyone to perform at your party, preview the act. If that's not feasible, ask to see a video or listen to a tape. Look beyond mere talent for stage presence and how the performer interacts with the audience. What counts is how your guests will enjoy the show.

IDEAS to MAKE it
Easy

—✳—

1 Recall past events for **inspiration:** What did your guests devour and what did they hide under the steak bones? **2** Don't try to **impress** guests with exotic foods if you know their tastes extend only to meat and potatoes. **3** **Round out** your menu with a few specialties from a take-out shop—but always taste before you buy. **4** Create an entire meal from dishes you've **made ahead** and stored in the refrigerator or freezer. All you have to do is heat and serve. **5** Collect one-pot recipes. You'll **save cooking time** and you'll satisfy even the most hearty appetites. **6** For a sit-down meal, have all food **ready** for serving before guests take their places at the table. **7** Sort your **shopping list** according to type of store. Try not to go to more than three. **8** Set out only the pieces of silverware you need for each table setting—you'll have **less to wash** and put away later. **9** **Disguise** ho-hum platters with fresh leaves, flower petals, or paper doilies. ●

CREATING THE MENU

CHOOSING NO-FUSS DISHES
THAT MAKE THE MEAL

⸻ ✳ ⸻

Breaking bread with friends is one of life's greatest joys. Preparing the bread can be one of life's more stressful experiences—but it doesn't have to be. A few tricks can spell the difference between looking forward to a meal and dreading it.

First, identify exactly what you like about entertaining. Is cooking a therapeutic experience for you? Do you feel pride when you see happy faces reflecting satisfied appetites? Or does the food itself take second place to designing a table filled with your favorite crystal, silver, and china?

Next, build a simple menu. If you're an expert only at grilling gourmet burgers, purchase other courses or ask guests to bring side dishes. Can't be bothered to spend time in the kitchen but care about esthetics? Buy a full-course meal from a restaurant and serve it on your English bone china. The secret is to do what you like best—it's that easy.

A Less-Stress Menu

WHEN YOU SIT DOWN TO PLAN YOUR MENU, DON'T CONVINCE YOURSELF THAT IT HAS TO COMPETE WITH A MEAL YOU'D ORDER AT A THREE-STAR RESTAURANT IN PARIS. INSTEAD, SIMPLY ASK YOURSELF WHAT YOU LIKE TO COOK.

Think about the kind of food you eat every day, the amount of time you spend in the kitchen, and how much effort you normally devote to putting food on the dinner table. Do you usually rip open a bag of prepared greens, pour them into a bowl, and top them with some tomatoes, croutons, and bottled dressing? Just dress up that same salad for your guests. Pick up a few loaves of breads at the best bakery in town and add one or two locally produced cheeses and a fine bottle of wine. Finish off the evening with freshly ground coffee and a store-bought dessert.

BEING REALISTIC

Maybe you seize every excuse to entertain because it gives you a chance to expand your culinary repertoire, and yet you still sweat bullets when the doorbell rings. What if you pour all your energy into this meal and everybody hates it? Not to worry: There are ways to head off anxiety attacks. Begin by asking yourself which dishes went over particularly well at past parties and which ones ended up as leftovers. List them in two columns on a sheet of paper.

Do people still talk about the lasagna you served two years ago, but only murmur politely when you ask how they liked last Sunday's apple pie? Be fair with yourself. Weren't you the only one who noticed that your salad dressing had too much vinegar in it? Didn't your guests devour the pasta that you thought needed more sauce? Wasn't that too-rare steak perfect for everyone but you?

Now move forward. What are you in the mood to eat? What do you really feel like cooking? Are you itching to make some fancy new concoction? Why? Is it

Estimating Portion Sizes

Figure on half a pound (250g) of meat per person, one-half to one cup (125–250ml) each of carbohydrates and vegetables, and one cup (250ml) of salad. If you're serving just hors d'oeuvres, plan on eight per hour per person.

because you want to experiment with an ethnic cuisine you've been reading about? Or do you want to impress your friends?

If you simply want to try something you haven't eaten before, save that desire and fulfill it in a restaurant. Or make the dish and test it on your family first. But if you want to be sure to impress your guests, serve them something that you can whip up with your eyes closed—and add store-bought items to round it out.

> If you want to be sure to impress your guests, serve them something you can whip up with your eyes closed.

You can serve a fabulous menu without draining your bank account or trying your patience. There's an old adage that says it's the first and last courses that count the most because they're the only ones anybody remembers. If you have one special dish in your repertoire that always wins rave reviews, serve it first or last.

Build a simple meal *around tacos, letting guests add their own toppings to the meat filling. Provide salsa, beans, and cheese.*

Otherwise, buy the best hors d'oeuvres you can find and then do the same for dessert. The middle course can be something as simple as a store-bought lasagna, a pot of chili, or a homey meat loaf.

HOW TO CHOOSE

When you sit down to plan a dinner party, does your mind go blank? Never fear: Whether you're a kitchen novice or an old hand, here are ways to jump-start your menu planning.

First, balance colors and textures. Second, don't repeat ingredients or food groups. Consider this well-rounded menu: a crunchy green salad; roasted red pepper soup; pasta with tender morsels of salmon and freshly picked green beans; and rich, chewy chocolate brownies. Or try this smorgasbord of finger foods: crisp, multi-colored raw vegetables; hummus with pita bread quarters; flaky crackers with a soft cheese; and sugar cookies for dessert.

WORKING WITHIN LIMITS

Next, think about whom you're feeding and what they like. If your meat-and-potatoes-loving in-laws are coming over for Sunday dinner, don't try to impress them with a Moroccan couscous. They'll be much happier with roasted chicken, mashed potatoes, and gravy.

The world is full of people with restricted diets, due to religious convictions, vegetarian leanings, or allergies to everything from milk to strawberries. Don't let them cramp your style. Be prepared with at least one dish that even the most particular guest will devour. Keep a stash of hot dogs and buns in the freezer for picky kids. Vegetarians are likely to relish pasta dressed with organic olive oil, herbs, and fresh-ground pepper. You probably have all those ingredients on hand.

Now examine your kitchen's limitations. When you think about your menu, analyze the size of your oven, the number of burners on your stove, how much counter space you have, and the capacity of your freezer and refrigerator. To avoid an appliance traffic jam, opt for variety: Serve a combination of stove-top, baked, room-temperature, and cold foods.

Now think about how you will serve your meal. If you plan a buffet and guests will sit with plates in their laps or they'll eat standing, avoid foods they'll need to slice or cut on their plates. Everything they eat should be manageable with a fork. Likewise, avoid serving sticky foods or things that will leave a stain if spilled. People who balance plates are typically more prone to accidents.

If guests will be seated at your dinner table for a family-style meal, avoid a table bulging with platters and bowls. Be sure that a serving of each food will fit on one dinner plate. That way you won't need to remove plates for each course.

Last but not least, when you plan your menu, honor your budget. Save money by tracking what you purchased for a previous party. Use it as your guideline to gauge what you're going to need for the next one. Note such things as how much food and drink was consumed and how many packages of party napkins were used.

It's easy to splurge at the store, but spending more than you can afford puts a damper on even the best of parties. If your pocketbook rebels at steak, buy hamburger. If dessert means more to you than wine, check out the sale wines and save funds for fresh raspberries and gourmet ice cream. Do what works for you and it will probably work for your guests as well.

Buy Precut Foods

For a super timesaver, buy produce and meat that has already been cleaned, chopped—even marinated. It's more expensive but well worth the prep time you'll save. Many supermarkets sell packages of prewashed and precut lettuces, spinach, and fancy mixed salads; prechopped cauliflower and broccoli; and marinated meat.

No-Fuss Food

---✳---

FEEDING PARTY GUESTS DOESN'T MEAN YOU HAVE TO SPEND WEEKS PORING OVER MAGAZINES AND COOKBOOKS, DAYS SHOPPING FOR INGREDIENTS, OR HOURS ERECTING ELABORATE CULINARY CONSTRUCTIONS.

Nor does it mean that when the big night arrives you must banish yourself to the kitchen for the duration while everyone else makes merry in the living room. Remember, spending time with you means far more to your guests than savoring the food on their plates.

RELIABLE DISHES

Follow the lead of many an experienced party giver and be eclectic. Have some reliable, ready-made star attractions that you can simply pull out of the freezer. Then raid the local gourmet shop or place an order for an assortment of entrées from one of your favorite restaurants.

Start by getting out your tried-and-true recipe. Everybody has one: the recipe that's been passed down from one cook to another for untold generations. Whether it's for chocolate-chip cookies, Irish stew, or eggplant parmigiana, you feel confident about this one dish. Even if you come from a family of noncooks, chances are you know how to make something your guests will love. If all you know is macaroni and cheese, you can still succeed (after all, isn't that everyone's ultimate comfort food?). Add a simple green salad, a basket of warm rolls, and a bottle of red wine. Finish it with root-beer floats and you're set. Your guests will love it.

Avoid experimenting when you're cooking for guests.

JUST ADD AN APPETIZER AND A ZESTY
PASTA, AND THIS IS A FULL MEAL.

Marinated Vegetable Salad

*This crunchy vegetable salad provides a shock
of color and texture. Allow time to marinate for
12 hours. Use prepackaged cut vegetables to save
preparation time.*

- 3 cups (750ml) each, broccoli and
  cauliflower florets
- 2 cups (500ml) baby carrots
- 2 small red bell peppers, seeds and veins
  discarded, cut into $^{1}/_{2}$-inch (12mm) strips
- 2 tablespoons grainy mustard
- $^{1}/_{2}$ cup (125ml) champagne vinegar
- 2 tablespoons granulated sugar
- $^{1}/_{2}$ teaspoon each, salt and pepper
- 1 cup (250ml) olive oil
- 2 tablespoons chopped fresh chives

Fill a large saucepan with salted water. Bring
to a boil over medium-high heat. Add the
broccoli and cauliflower. Cook for 1 minute,
or until broccoli turns bright green. Remove
vegetables with a slotted spoon, and drain.
Repeat with carrots, cooking them for 2 to
3 minutes. Combine vegetables in a large
bowl. In a small bowl, whisk together the
mustard, vinegar, sugar, salt, and pepper.
Gradually add the oil, whisking until well
incorporated. Pour the vinaigrette over the
vegetables and toss to coat evenly. Marinate,
refrigerated, at least 12 hours. Garnish with
fresh chives right before serving. **Serves 8**

Then there are the newer favorites you've
been making a lot lately. You come upon
a recipe in a magazine or a cookbook, you
try it, and it's love at first bite. You make
it over and over and over because it's so
good and easy to prepare. Serve it to your
guests. They will never know that you ate
it every day last week.

If cooking the same dish repeatedly
makes you squeamish, take the in-between
approach. Cook one or two of your favorite
recipes and buy premade side dishes to
complete the menu. If you're celebrated
throughout the neighborhood for your
barbecued chicken, for instance, serve it
with crunchy bread and an assortment of
pasta and potato salads from the local market. Serve with beer or white wine.

ONE-POT MEALS

The various dishes that can be cooked in
one pot are often far less time-consuming
to prepare than are entrées with several
side dishes. From sophisticated cassoulets
to your basic chili, from traditional hearty
soups and stews to delectable paellas, the
one-pot main dish certainly ranks among
the world's great inventions.

There is something truly comforting
about food slowly simmered in a single
vessel, served steaming hot in an ample,
thick-walled ceramic bowl. Add some
fresh bread, a salad, cheese, and a baked
tart for a touch of elegance.

Cooks love all-in-one concoctions
as much as guests do, because they can
just toss everything into one container,
put it on the range top or pop it into the
oven, and maybe stir it now and then.

Should extra guests show up, one-pot meals are easily shared—just fill in with extra bread or toss some more salad.

You can make even the most humble casserole the star attraction of a dinner party: just add soup, a steamed vegetable, and a simple dessert such as a store-bought apple pie or cheesecake.

MAKE-AHEAD MEALS

You can also cut down on menu anxiety by making meals ahead. Cookbooks, magazines, and newspapers are chock-full of recipes you can make ahead of time. On rainy weekends or whenever the cooking mood strikes, throw together a casserole, make a pot of chili, or whip up some salsa, pesto, or chutney (it's easier than you think). Fill your fridge, freezer, and pantry with the products of your labors.

When unexpected guests arrive (or when you want to spend time with your guests and not in front of the stove) simply pull out an entrée, defrost it, heat, and serve. Your microwave can help you get these tasks done in a few minutes. Even the classic accompaniments—vegetables, bread, and dessert—can be frozen and defrosted for such emergencies.

SELF-SERVE MEALS

Here's another idea: self-serve menus. Everyone loves to create their own meal when someone else has done all the prep work. Set out bowls of fixings for salads or sandwiches and let everyone have at it. Or serve a festive Mexican meal: Invite your guests to stuff taco shells and tortillas with their favorite fillings.

◆

Sundae in a Cup

Frozen puff pastry (sold in the frozen-food section of most grocery stores) is one of the simplest ways to achieve superb desserts with little effort. Try this old-time favorite served with a new twist.

- ◆ 1¹/2 cups (375ml) premium chocolate sauce (or see recipe below)
- ◆ 8 premade and baked puff pastry shells (follow package directions)
- ◆ 2 pints (1L) premium vanilla ice cream
- ◆ 2 cups (500ml) fresh raspberries
- ◆ Fresh mint (for garnish)
- ◆ Whipped cream (optional)

Drizzle ¹/4 cup (50ml) of the chocolate sauce over each plate (or save to drizzle on top of the ice cream). Place a large scoop of ice cream in each pastry shell. Garnish with raspberries and a sprig of mint (add a dollop of whipped cream, if desired). **Serves 8**

Premium store-bought chocolate sauce is fine, but here's a recipe for making your own chocolate sauce:

- ◆ 1 cup (250ml) heavy cream
- ◆ 9 ounces (250g) good-quality bittersweet chocolate (chips or finely chopped)
- ◆ 1 tablespoon (15ml) vanilla extract

Bring the cream to a soft boil in a heavy pot over medium-low heat. Stir in the chocolate and continue to stir until completely melted. Add the vanilla. Serve immediately, or refrigerate for later use. Reheat when ready to serve. **Makes 1¹/2 cups (375ml)**

A cheese course, *served with crackers, grapes, and glasses of port, is a simple-to-assemble addition to any menu.*

The serve-it-yourself meal has many benefits. For one thing, your guests can eat all they want, the way they like it. You also avoid the hassle of serving. You simply put your selections in attractive platters and bowls and set them out for easy access on the kitchen counter, preferably next to the stove, where casseroles or sauces can stay warm on the burners.

Gather Ingredients First

If you're working from a recipe, measure out each of the ingredients first. Line them up on the counter or table. When you have finished, begin assembling and mixing. This way, you can be sure that you aren't missing or duplicating any ingredients.

If you're still struggling with your menu, just follow the lead of master chefs from Santa Fe to Paris. Serve food at the peak of its growing season. It's hard to improve on homegrown summer tomatoes served sliced with mozzarella cheese, sprinkled with fresh basil, and drizzled with good olive oil. And what dessert could ever top garden-picked berries or sliced peaches with fresh whipped cream? When the weather turns cold, douse winter squash with butter, add nutmeg and cinnamon, and pop it in the oven. Or cut up the leftover cooked squash, toss in a handful or two of chopped walnuts, and spoon the results over cooked pasta.

LAST-MINUTE PREP

If you plan an entire menu that you have to assemble at the last minute, it can be done. Here's how the restaurant pros do it: Cook each component separately in advance, then put everything together at the last minute. For example, boil pasta, toss it with oil, and set it aside for a few hours until you're ready to cover it with that reheated spicy tomato sauce you made and froze two weeks ago. Or do all of your prep work—peeling, chopping, grating, and slicing—early in the day and set the results aside to be put together during the final moments.

If you're not cooking, last-minute makeovers can improve prepared food you've brought in from elsewhere. Ready-made food has changed since the days when deli platters stood center stage at parties. If the very words make you think of disposable metal trays covered with thin layers of mystery lunch meat, limp lettuce, and processed cheese, think again. Even supermarkets are now more sophisticated, and have expanded their selections of party fare well beyond potato chips and dips, pretzels, and tortilla chips and salsa.

Here's the secret. Keep your pantry stocked with jars of Greek and Spanish olives, roasted red peppers, pepperoncini, pickled onions, and mushrooms. When an impromptu get-together beckons, pick up some cold cuts and dress them up with goodies from your party stash.

Or try an instant attractive appetizer like this: Fill small festive bowls with three or four different kinds of salsa, set them on a big wooden tray, and surround them with multicolored tortilla chips.

COHOSTING A PARTY

You may be wondering whether you have to do all this cooking and planning yourself. The answer: Of course not. Ask a friend to cohost a party with you. Sharing host responsibilities allows you to divide the cost and labor. It's an especially great idea if you and a friend have similar styles and complementary talents.

Decide what your menu will be and then divide the tasks equitably. Plan a buffet menu so you split the number of dishes that need to be prepared. Trade off courses so that one person is responsible for the appetizer and dessert and the other takes care of the hors d'oeuvres and main course. You could also split duties on beverages or supplies. Create a budget and pool your funds, or divide the expenses at the end when they are all tallied.

Joining forces with a friend can increase the potential for fun. Consider cohosting a baby shower or birthday bash. Or, throw a party simply because you enjoy working together. Invite your respective friends for an easy night of socializing.

SCHEDULING YOUR TASKS

Former U.S. President George Bush once said, "Uncertainty is the enemy." He probably wasn't referring to entertaining, but the principle is the same: The hardest thing to deal with in life is the unknown.

Fortunately, you're throwing a party, not running a country. Anticipating what needs to be done and when is a skill you can learn. Simply sit down and make a schedule that covers your time between now and the day of the party.

Having a clear strategy will not only help you work more efficiently, but will also keep you from forgetting anything—

SIMPLY PUT...

COURSES

hors d'oeuvres • Served with cocktails before a meal. Usually consist of finger foods or small portions.

appetizer • A small course served before a meal, or as the first course.

entrée, main course • Dish or dishes served as the main part of the meal. These often consist of meat, poultry, or fish, or can be vegetarian.

Proper scheduling means you'll be
ready to party by the time guests arrive.

like those few extra chairs, that special
brand of root beer you meant to buy for
the kids, or the cake that somehow didn't
get ordered in time.

Take cooking time into account. Your
goal could be to put everything on a buffet table at once, or to serve the appetizer,
salad, main dish, and dessert in succession
as guests are seated at the dinner table. A
stuffed pork roast takes more than twice
as long to cook as a marinated pork loin,
so plan accordingly. You can stir-fry strips
of chicken in a snap, but roasting a whole
bird will take longer.

Now that you've decided what's on
the menu, you can jot down everything
that needs to be done pertaining to food
and drink. Include orders on any needed
rentals, shopping, do-ahead preparation,
requests for borrowed items, and last-
minute tasks. Pay special attention to the
details like defrosting, garnishing, and
washing seldom-used glasses and plates.

Next to each entry write down how far in
advance you can do it. For sanity's sake,
compare your list with your calendar. Are
some days already so packed they can't
accommodate one more thing? Block
them out. Make a countdown from the
day you start your planning (see opposite

**Your goal could be to put every
dish on a buffet table at once, or to
serve each in succession as guests
are seated at the dinner table.**

page). Then divide the tasks evenly among
the number of days remaining, trying not
to save any major chores for the very last
minute. This approach will spread out the
work and make it seem more manageable.
Be realistic with your goals; everything
will end up taking longer than you think.
But with a little planning, you'll have a
system that really works.

COUNTDOWN TO A DINNER PARTY

---✶---

A MEAL PLANNED WELL AND COOKED on a timetable is nearly fool-proof. The secret is to stagger preparation. For a casual dinner party, plan to make a main course you can freeze weeks ahead and thaw the day before serving. All you have to do on party day is get last-minute supplies, prepare the hors d'oeuvres and salad, heat the main course, and organize dessert and coffee. Here's a typical timetable.

...one month out. Plan your menu; create your shopping list; inspect your plates, glasses, eating utensils, and serving pieces; reserve rental items (always order a few extra).

...two weeks prior. Shop for nonperishable food, including dried and frozen ingredients; buy alcoholic and nonalcoholic beverages; cook the main course and freeze it in an ovenproof container, all ready to be reheated.

...one week before. Wash any serving pieces, glasses, utensils, pitchers, or plates that you haven't used lately.

...three days prior. Assemble music tapes; prepare components of the dessert that you can make ahead; make the salad vinaigrette.

...the day before. Buy perishable foods; remove the main course from the freezer to thaw in the fridge; buy flowers and arrange them in a low centerpiece; set the table.

...the morning of the party. Shop for last-minute supplies such as ice, bread, and fresh herbs; peel, chop, and prepare the lettuce or vegetables for the salad. Cover the salad with a damp paper towel and store it in the fridge.

...in the afternoon. Prepare the remaining salad ingredients and add to the salad bowl; assemble the dessert and bake if required.

...two hours before. Make your final dessert preparations; slice the cheese and arrange it on a plate; fill the coffeepot with water and set up the filter and coffee; preheat the oven; place the thawed main course in the oven and let it bake at a low temperature.

...one hour before. Arrange hors d'oeuvres on platters. Fill a pitcher with ice cubes and water; open the white wine, recork it, and keep it chilled in an ice bucket. Set out glasses.

...when guests arrive. Greet your guests at the door and offer each of them a glass of wine; remove the main course from the oven and let it sit on top of the stove, covered, until dinner (about 30 minutes).

...15 minutes before dinner. Remove the salad from the refrigerator; heat and slice the bread; uncork the red wine; fill water glasses; add vinaigrette to the salad and toss it; place bread in a basket and set it out along with butter and cheese.

...dinnertime. Place the salad on the dining table; transfer the main course to a serving platter and garnish it with fresh chopped herbs or seasonings; set out the main course on the table (don't forget to put the appropriate serving utensils with it); brew the coffee.

...during dinner. Refill wine and water glasses, offer second helpings; replenish any empty bread baskets or platters.

...after the main course. Clear the dinner plates off the table; divide the dessert among small plates and serve it; offer coffee. Sit back and relax. Wasn't that a snap?

You Don't Have to Cook

---✳︎---

B Y NOW YOU MAY HAVE MANY IDEAS ABOUT WHAT TO SERVE AT YOUR PARTY. IF YOU ARE STILL DRAWING BLANKS, HOWEVER, DON'T DESPAIR. HERE ARE SOME ELEGANT MENU IDEAS THAT INVOLVE PRACTICALLY NO COOKING AT ALL.

These ideas will also impress your guests out of all proportion to the time and talent required to make them.

You can find the ingredients in any gourmet food shop and many supermarkets. Short of a catastrophic spill, there's no way to ruin these dishes. Best of all, such foods add glamour to any menu.

Try one or two of the following dishes the next time you have guests, then smile and accept the applause: Steam asparagus, season it with salt and pepper, and top with crumbled feta cheese. Steam some artichokes and arrange them on a platter surrounded by lemon wedges and dishes of melted butter. Slice pears and serve with Stilton cheese and walnut bread. Boil a pot of fettuccine, toss it in a beautiful bowl with store-bought pesto and halved cherry tomatoes, and let your guests grate their own fresh Parmesan. Throw together a salad of romaine lettuce, hard-boiled

Have others prepare your meal, and serve it on your own dishes. Who's to know?

eggs, fresh dill, lemon juice, olive oil, salt, and pepper. Offer focaccia bread and tart apples with aged Asiago cheese. Make instant guacamole by mashing avocados with a good salsa. Create memorable spreads by mixing chopped vegetables or spices with plain yogurt or pureed beans. Or combine whipped cream cheese with sun-dried tomatoes or olive relish.

OUT OF THE KITCHEN

So, you've thought about what you'd like to serve, and the bottom line is, you don't want to cook. No problem: You can serve your guests a great meal without so much as cracking open the fridge or turning on the stove. There are the obvious ways: Throw a cocktail party, complete with crackers and cheese, or chips and dip. Or invite old friends to catch up over coffee and a cake from the bakery. But believe it or not, it's also possible to host an elegant full-course dinner without even lifting a spoon. Consider these options:

Entertain at a restaurant. Can't beat it—you don't have to cook; you don't have to clean up, either before the party or after; and everyone chooses what he or she wants, so you don't have to give a thought to finicky eaters. It doesn't have to be an expensive proposition. There are easy ways to beat the costs at all but the priciest eatery in town. First, the obvious: You can choose an inexpensive restaurant—every community has its bargain spots, from neighborhood bistros and pizza parlors to family-run Mexican cantinas and Italian trattorias. If you go to a midrange restaurant, you'll save money if

Serve a bountiful buffet *with takeout from your local supermarket, restaurant, or deli. Add breads, olives, pickles, and other condiments for a robust no-cook repast.*

you choose three entrées from a fixed-price menu, then let your guests select from among your choices. Liquor makes the bill rise fast. Serve cocktails at home before dinner, or take your own wine to the restaurant. (Most restaurants allow

Slice pears and serve with Stilton cheese and walnut bread. Or make instant guacamole by mashing avocados with a good salsa.

you to do this; though they may charge a corkage fee, the total cost will be far less than the cost of ordering bottles off the house wine list. Call to check.)

Serve takeout. Stay home and pick up wonderful dishes. Today, more restaurants than ever before offer food to go, and it's no longer limited to just hamburgers or Chinese food. Pick up containers of pasta and sauce from an Italian trattoria and toss them together when you're ready to eat. Or drop into an Indian or Thai restaurant for a collection of white cartons filled with assorted delicacies. Serve these piping hot in delicate Asian pottery.

Even that old standby, pizza, has gone upscale. Baked in wood-fired ovens and embellished with toppings ranging from home-ground sausage to goat cheese to

Try home replacement meals. If you're wondering what exactly that means, it's the new buzzword of the food industry and it's aimed at you—the host who wants to serve a full meal but doesn't have time to cook. Many supermarkets and gourmet food stores have a wide selection of fully cooked main courses and side dishes that

Entertaining isn't just about dinner. Invite guests over for a pitcher of margaritas and tortilla chips. Or hold a cookie swap.

portobello mushrooms, it's worthy of all but the most formal dinner party. You may not even have to pick up the food. Most major cities have couriers who deliver menu items from an array of good restaurants; look in the Yellow Pages.

Invite guests to an easy *alfresco European lunch. Just provide artisan breads, cheeses, dressed salad greens, figs, and grapes.*

simply need reheating. Always ask for a taste before buying something to take home for company. Back in your own kitchen, don't be afraid to add a few of your own touches, including a little extra seasoning or an herb garnish. Transfer the store-bought dishes to your own serving pieces. Once it's on your table, who's to know you haven't been slaving away?

Have a potluck dinner. Before the days of take-out shops and dinner-delivery services, potluck meals were your primary option if you wanted to have people over for dinner but you didn't want to cook. It works just as well today. You supply the drinks and store-bought appetizers; your guests bring the rest. Tell people to bring whatever they like, or, if you like more control, assign a specific dish to each person. Be sure to warn guests of your kitchen's limitations, and ask them what they'll need in the way of serving pieces and kitchen equipment.

A bring-your-own-food party offers a variation on the potluck theme. All you have to do is buy some side dishes and fire up the grill or the oven. The guests bring and cook whatever they want to eat.

INSTEAD OF DINNER

If you're bored with the idea of having people over for a meal, don't despair: Entertaining isn't just about dinner.

Why not invite your guests over for a pitcher of margaritas and tortilla chips?

Hold a dessert or cookie swap. Guests bring goodies to sample and to take home; you provide the venue and beverages.

Build your party around a game or an activity—toss a football at the beach, hike in the woods, play a game of badminton in the backyard or poker by the fire.

Invite friends over to watch a couple of classic videos after dinner. Offer them drinks and bowls of popcorn.

When you want to catch up with the neighbors, ask them over for a simple glass of iced tea on the back porch.

A well-stocked PANTRY

FILL YOUR PANTRY WITH THE FOODS YOU SERVE GUESTS MOST OFTEN. BUY SMALLER AMOUNTS OF WHAT WON'T STAY FRESH AND LARGER SUPPLIES OF VERSATILE NONPERISHABLES.

Ready accompaniments

Stock ingredients that can be combined to create an entire dish for impromptu entertaining, or that work well for last-minute snacks. Jars of salsas, pasta sauces, roasted red peppers, and sun-dried tomatoes can be mixed with pasta, spread on crackers, or mixed into dip for crudités. Keep olive oils and vinegars (especially balsamic) on hand for enhancing salads, as a dip for bread, or as a topping for pasta.

Side dishes in a flash

Store items that need only to be doctored, heated, or cooked. Soup is an ideal starter on a cold night. Canned black beans are great as a side dish. Stash packages of dry goods that need little preparation—pasta, rice mixes, and couscous cook in minutes.

Spicing up a meal

Keep a variety of herbs and spices to enhance everything from home replacement meals to premade sauces. Mix curry powder with plain yogurt for a dip, or stir it into sauces and stews. Add a little fire to a premade sauce with chili powder. An Italian seasoning blend adds flavor to bland meals.

SMART SHOPPING

---✳---

Finding time to shop is stressful enough. Add the inevitable traffic jams on the road, in the aisles, and at the checkout counter, and it's enough to send your blood pressure through the roof.

Fortunately, there are ways to get everything you need—from hors d'oeuvre trays to after-dinner drinks—without driving yourself crazy in the process.

The first step on the road to efficiency is to make lists and organize them. Write down everything you need, including the quantity. Sort your entries according to which stores (the bakery, the supermarket, the hardware store) carry what products. Within each store list, divide the items by category. For instance, your supermarket list might include headings for produce, baked goods, beverages, dairy products, and meat. Sorting by category within a store might seem like overkill, but think again: Visiting one large, comprehensive store can be overwhelming. You don't want to waste your precious time running up and down the aisles in a random fashion, frantically looking for something.

SIMPLE STRATEGIES

Stick with stores you know. Finding what you want quickly can save you valuable time. Get to know the people at the stores you frequent. They'll make your shopping trips faster and more pleasant.

Shop during off-hours. Don't hit the supermarket on your way home from work. If your daily routine is flexible, shop early in the morning, when there are fewer shoppers and the staff is stocking the shelves. Not only will you avoid the crowds, but you'll also get to buy the freshest meat and produce. The second-best time is after dinner, but don't wait long: In the evening, stock can run low and special departments like the seafood counter and the bakery may be closed.

Chart your course. If you're making one marathon shopping spree, map your route from store to store, planning steps in the most logical order. If you're spreading out your trips, choose stores you can visit in the course of your routine travels.

Find ways to shop from home. You probably think nothing of picking up the phone to order a Christmas present from

Take a Cooler Chest

If you're shopping at more than one store, especially on a warm day, take along an ice-filled cooler. Keeping dairy products, meat, fish, and fresh produce chilled not only prevents spoilage but also can fend off food-borne illnesses. Prevent spoilage by wrapping items well so juices do not mingle.

a catalog. Why not do the same for your next supply of party food? Your mailbox no doubt yields many gourmet food and kitchen catalogs. Keep a few on hand and comb them for possibilities. You can also see if any grocery stores in your area have Web sites, as it's now possible to order food and supplies over the Internet.

Get to know the people who work in the stores you frequent. They'll make your shopping trips faster and more pleasant.

Use delivery services. Find a grocery store that accepts phone or fax orders—most cities have at least a few. Or call a grocery-delivery or errand-running service. Check the index of your local phone book under "Shopping Services" or "Food Delivery." And when you order, especially if it's near one of the major holidays, be sure to find out about turnaround times.

Ask for help. If you just don't have time to shop, ask someone else to do it for you. Perhaps you know a neighboring teenager who would be happy to take on the chore in exchange for the admission price to a couple of movies. Would your significant other be willing to stop at the store on the way home from work? Can your mother pick up a few things for you while she's doing her own shopping?

BUDGETING WISELY

Entertaining can be a costly undertaking, but there's no need to overspend. When you're buying in larger quantities than normal—and probably buying items you don't normally use—watch your wallet. Fortunately, it's easy to pinch pennies without compromising quality. If there's time before your party, stock up on necessities when they're on sale.

Produce stands *can be handy if they're close to home or work. Ask the staff to recommend the freshest fruits and vegetables.*

To make grocery shopping *efficient, don't visit the supermarket on your way home from work. Instead, shop during off-hours.*

Even for an impromptu event there are lots of ways to save: Discount and warehouse stores sell almost anything you can think of in large quantities and at low prices. Coupons from newspapers, magazines, and direct-mail booklets can save more money than you might expect. Picking up that

Premium food is often worth the expense; it's virtually guaranteed to be more flavorful than its bargain-basement counterpart.

extra-large box or buying from the bulk bins usually costs less; it's perfect for those times when you need large quantities of pasta, rice, or dried foods. You'll also find great food at lower-than-supermarket prices in ethnic or farmers' markets.

Bargains can be exhilarating but they're not always appropriate. Be wary of purchasing perishable products that have an expiration date only a few days away. Although they may have attractive prices, these products are likely to spoil before you can use them—especially if you're buying in bulk. Then you will need to buy replacements, thus paying double and spending twice as much time shopping. Also assess the condition of any fresh produce. Ripe produce is great, but only if you plan to use the fruits and vegetables that day or the next.

QUALITY OR QUANTITY

Buying top-of-the-line food might not sound like a way to save time and money, but it often is. A premium product is virtually guaranteed to be more flavorful than its bargain-basement counterpart. A macaroni salad at the supermarket might have a low price tag, but chances are it will be so bland that you'll doctor it with herbs, onions, maybe some olives—and wind up spending more than you would have if you'd bought the expensive stuff at the gourmet deli. The same holds true for any exotic spices or other special ingredients that a recipe may require. It's always better to seek out the real thing than to settle for inexpensive substitutes that may prove to be disappointing.

Finally, determine quantity carefully. Leftovers at the end of a party are wonderful; needless excess is not. When you're making your shopping list, estimate quantities as closely as you can. Buy only what you need; avoid waste and the need to send your guests home with bags and plates of leftovers. By the same token, don't buy too little. If you run short of ingredients, you may end up making a desperate last-minute trip to the store.

SERVICE WITH STYLE

---✳---

THE WAY YOU SERVE YOUR MEAL IS A MATTER OF INDIVIDUAL STYLE, BUT YOU'RE MORE LIKELY TO MAKE IT A GREAT SUCCESS IF YOU KEEP A FEW THINGS IN MIND. FIRST, DECIDE HOW BEST TO SERVE YOUR MEAL.

Look at how much space is at your disposal and how willing you are to scavenge extra chairs, seat people at makeshift tables, or make space on the floor.

A formal sit-down dinner for two is romantic, for four is intimate, for eight is sophisticated. But for 20 it's usually impractical, and it may be a recipe for a nervous breakdown. For large groups or small spaces a buffet usually works best. Or meet in the middle with a good old family-style dinner, where everything is laid out on the table at the start.

If you have your heart set on a formal sit-down dinner for more than eight people, hire a caterer if you can afford it, or plan dishes that are already prepared. Even for just six or eight, a sit-down dinner is the most stress-inducing form of entertaining. Have someone else do the service and cleanup if you possibly can, even if it's only the teenager next door, a local college student, or your friendly babysitter. If you must go it alone or with minimal help, you'll need to plan your menu and your timing very carefully.

Prepare everything for serving before your guests take their places around the table. Start with a cold appetizer you can put on plates long before anyone arrives, and keep it at room temperature or store it in the refrigerator until serving time. Get all of the necessary plates and bowls ready. Apply all the garnishes and trimmings in advance. To avoid having to cook between courses, keep soups simmering

If you're expecting a large crowd, prepare extra seating for guests.

on the stove top, side dishes and grilled foods and other entrées warming in the oven, and salads ready and waiting so you can add dressing at the last minute.

EASY BUFFETS

Without a doubt, a buffet is the easiest way to serve a crowd. Guests can help themselves, then saunter off to locations that please them. Chairs, couches, beds,

fabric; and surround them with greens, flowers or potted plants, candles, even whole fruits and vegetables.

The best buffets look abundant. More is always better than less—no one wants to take the last bite. Have extra food on hand so you can refill bowls and platters as soon as they're emptied. If something runs out, remove the empty dish and replace it with more of something else.

If your table can't hold all the food, it's easy to make a sideboard out of a card table or pine boards on boxes, all covered with a cloth.

and floors all become acceptable seating, and any flat surface, from a lap to a coffee table, can hold a plate.

To further simplify your party, prepare your serving table early. Decide where everything will go. Make the table visually exciting by adding risers: Simply arrange phone books, wooden blocks, or upended cake pans on the table; disguise them with

Plan the setup to keep traffic flowing. Clear a path around the table so people can move around it freely. Start with the plates at one end and finish with napkins and eating utensils at the other. Serve

A sit-down meal *can be simple if you serve it family style, with everything on the table. Balance make-ahead dishes with those that can be assembled at the last minute.*

foods that people can spoon out using one hand while they hold their plates in the other, or make sure there's enough room for them to set down their plates while they serve themselves.

FAMILY-STYLE SERVICE

If you have enough room for all of your guests to gather around your dining table, the simplest solution is a family-style dinner. If the table can't hold all the food and you don't have a sideboard, it's easy to make one out of a card table or a couple of pine boards on boxes. Cover it with cloth—a large solid-colored flat sheet will work—and park your serving dishes there until it's time to pass them around.

Watch out for spills, and make sure platters are neither too heavy nor too hot to handle. If you entertain this way often, or plan to, you might want to invest in a lazy Susan that guests can spin to reach distant dishes, or a warming tray to keep foods hot on the sideboard.

THE TABLE SETTING

Setting your dining table should be fun, not another source of stress. If you can't remember which fork goes where, which type of glass to use for what, and how to fold a napkin, don't worry. There are creative solutions to everything. Besides, Emily Post isn't coming to your party.

Start with the table. Whether it's your great-grandmother's Chippendale dining table or a sheet of plywood balanced on sawhorses, make sure it's clean and level. If it's a beautiful piece of furniture, whether old or new, show it off. If that

THE MORE DISTINCTIVE AND APPEALING A SERVING DISH IS ON ITS OWN, THE LESS GARNISH YOU'LL NEED.

◇

Colorful beauties

These platters are ideal for casual buffets and family-style meals. Mix and match patterns and colors. Hang them on the wall when not in use. Be aware that some imported and antique dishes may have lead content and therefore are unsafe for food.

Formal white china

Elegant, sleek platters of white china with a gold or silver trim are ideal for formal events. Secondhand and antique stores are treasure troves of platters with classic trims.

Varied shapes and sizes

Collect uniquely shaped platters to compensate for nondescript tableware. Showcase different or unique shapes: square, rectangle, and star are a few variations. Japanese pottery, for example, comes in a wide variety of shapes and colors.

Colored glassware

Use glass pieces in assorted colors. Textured plates are especially pretty. Look for glass platters trimmed with a decorative metallic finish or clear glass that has been coated or impregnated with an iridescent sheen. Avoid glassware with painted-on designs; these could flake off and get into food.

DECORATIVE LINENS

TABLECLOTHS, PLACE MATS, AND napkins add texture and vibrancy to a table setting. Pair vintage linens with paper products. Layer heavy damask with delicate lace. Mix bright solids with bold prints. Let your imagination be your guide.

Use bandannas *or other unusual fabric pieces as napkins. Complete the look with imaginative napkin rings of string and chilis.*

Lay down *squares of butcher paper and let guests decorate their own place settings.*

For buffets, *roll flatware inside colorful napkins, tie a ribbon around each, and arrange in a basket or pail.*

Double up *on tablecloths for a lush look. Use contrasting colors or patterns. Gather the corners of the top cloth, and tie with ribbon or raffia.*

makes you nervous, protect the surface from burns, spills, and scratches. If you plan to cover it with a tablecloth, use a felt pad or plastic liner underneath. Or set plates and serving dishes on trivets, place mats, or cutting boards.

If your table is makeshift, or if you want it to match the mood of your party, cover it. A strictly formal dinner might warrant an elegant linen tablecloth. For a dressy affair choose fancy linens (you can find them at antique shops and thrift stores). For a casual meal, your options are limitless. Department and housewares stores, even large supermarkets, sell attractive place mats. Or make your own using decorative paper or swatches of fabric.

Anything goes, from a Dublin linen tablecloth to a colorful woolen blanket or fabric remnants you've found at the thrift store. Even yesterday's newspaper will work if you're serving fresh-boiled crab or lobster and you want to mimic the atmosphere of a seaside café.

CENTERPIECE DRAMA

By far the easiest way to create whimsy, drama, or elegance for your table setting is to whip up a fabulous centerpiece. You can never go wrong with flowers. Purchase flowering plants from a garden center and tuck them into a big wicker basket. Or clip single buds—dahlias, cosmos, and roses— from your garden and cluster them, each in its own glass bottle or bud vase, in the middle of the table.

Beyond flowers, nothing adds atmosphere like candles. Use colors that will enhance or complement your table setting.

Display your favorite *flowered china at your next brunch or afternoon tea. It's also fun to mix and match assorted patterns of dishes.*

Or use colors to reflect the occasion, season, or holiday. Use a variety of heights and diameters. Place candles on mirrors, in decorative glasses, or in hollowed-out fresh fruits and vegetables. Be sure to use dripless candles, or be prepared to scrape wax off linens and tabletops. Avoid using scented candles, especially near food or in the presence of allergy-prone guests.

If your table is makeshift, cover it. Anything goes, from a Dublin linen tablecloth to a colorful woolen blanket or fabric remnants you've found at the thrift store.

Centerpieces are easy. Just use anything that strikes your fancy: piled seasonal fruits and vegetables, flowering dwarf trees, holiday decorations, even toys. Whatever you use, make sure it's low enough to see over or tall enough to see under. Nothing is more frustrating than trying to talk to someone who's hidden behind a mountain of flowers and fruit.

Crystal glasses sparkle at a table set for a formal meal. Use one glass for water and one for each type of wine you're serving.

PLACE-SETTING IDEAS

When it comes to place settings, these days almost anything goes. And the simplest approach is to use whatever you have. If your grandmother left you a full set of china, you can use the whole set, down to the bread plates and demitasse cups. Haul out the floral plates you've collected for

fewer choices your guests have to make. If you clear dishes between courses and your guests have set their utensils on their plates, simply return the utensils to their original places on the table before you clear the used plates away.

A technically proper table setting will probably be the last thing on your guests' minds. Still, it's reassuring to get things right. Knives and spoons go on the right, with the knives closer to the plate, blade

Even a flat tin pan or a plastic plate can be beautiful if you disguise it. Cover the surface with a napkin or fresh grape leaves.

years and mix them with the earthenware bowls you bought at a craft fair. Or buy colorful paper plates for a casual dinner and simplify your cleanup.

When you set out silverware, less is more. Fewer pieces on the table mean fewer for you to wash and put away, and

edges facing in. Put forks on the left, with the fork for the first course on the outside. The dessert fork and spoon are at the top of the place setting, turned parallel with the table edge. (When in doubt, remember that the first utensils to be used go on the outside.) If all this seems like too much fuss, bundle everything inside napkins, tie a ribbon around each bundle, and place one in the center of each plate.

Few sights are more festive than a table set with sparkling glassware. Don't worry if things don't match—diversity of color and shape only adds to the festivity. If you have enough glasses and enough room on the table, set out everything at once. You'll want a glass for water and one for each kind of wine you're serving. As in the case of silver, the glass to be used first goes to the right of any other glasses.

If you have beautiful plates and dishes, use them. Take your collection of cut-glass candy dishes off the shelf and fill them with dips or herb-blended butters. Stand bread sticks in your favorite Portuguese pottery mugs. Get out the lead-free crystal punch bowl you haven't seen since your wedding day and toss a huge salad in it.

USING VISUAL TRICKS

What if you don't have wonderful treasures lurking in your cupboards? What if you don't even have nice-looking platters? Not to worry: Sleight of hand can come to the rescue. A mirror can make a great serving platter. So can a big ceramic tile. And even a flat tin pan or a plastic plate can look beautiful if you disguise it. Simply cover the surface with a napkin and no one will be the wiser. Or go one creative step further and use sliced lemons or fresh grape leaves, a bed of colorful lettuce, or herbs as a decorative border.

If you need inspiration, think of architecture, sculpture, and dance. All three of these art forms fascinate because

of the ways in which they blend height, shape, and texture. You can lay out a stunning collection of antique sterling silver platters, but if they're all round and flat your table will look dull. Instead, combine tall, footed glass bowls with rectangular silver trays; round ceramic platters with odd-shaped, textured glass plates; square bread baskets with oval tureens. Use a variety of sizes and materials.

SIMPLY PUT...

EFFORTLESS GARNISHES

coulis • Essentially a puree or sauce with one prominent ingredient, a coulis (pronounced cool-EE) can be sweet or savory. Spread it on a plate and place food on top, or drizzle it onto food. Try a strawberry coulis on angel food cake, or make a savory tomato-and-basil coulis as a sauce.

edible flowers • From whole nasturtiums to rose petals, these tasty, colorful treats add a beautiful touch. Look for edible blossoms in the produce department or at specialty stores, or gather them from your garden. Make sure they're free of sprayed-on pesticides or those added to the soil.

flowering kale • Sometimes called ornamental kale, this large head of frilly greens comes in variegated shades of green and purple or green and white. Spread the leaves on a plate to make a bed for all types of food.

PERSONALIZING PLACE SETTINGS MAKES A PARTY MEMORABLE. DON'T BOTHER WITH SPECIAL PROPS—EVEN THE ORDINARY CAN BE MADE INTERESTING.

Baked goods

Buy sugar cookies or bake prepared sugar-cookie dough into a desired shape. Write the guests' names using prepared icing.

Playful game pieces

For a touch of whimsy, spell out names with letters from a word game.

Seasonal produce

Use a gold pen to write names on lemon or lime leaves. Peel back the husk of an ear of corn and tuck a handwritten paper name card within. Or turn an artichoke into a card holder—cut off the bottom of the vegetable to make a flat edge and then slip the card between the leaves.

It's only natural to want everything to be perfect for your guests and to worry that your efforts won't quite be up to snuff. Ease your mind by remembering that no matter what kind of party you're having, sharing good times with people you like is more important than the food you serve or the china you use.

CLASSIC PRESENTATIONS

Tasty food is doubly appealing when it's beautifully presented. Think of presentation as similar to adding accessories to clothing: That black silk dress is attractive all by itself, but adding a string of pearls completes the look.

Don't let the idea of beautiful presentation overwhelm you. Enhancing the appearance of food doesn't mean you need to spend hours cutting radishes into roses. In fact, if you have neither the time nor the patience for fussing, simply pay attention to color and contrast. You'll be surprised at the difference it makes. If you don't believe it, just put some deep-red Bing cherries in a dark-blue bowl.

Make the day of the event easier and avoid last-minute stress by working in advance. Here are a few smart ways to make presentation easy—and attractive.

To minimize kitchen duty, arrange food on serving dishes as far in advance as you can. The more time you have, the less stressed you'll feel, whether you want to create a grand presentation or simply have everything ready when the guests arrive.

Wrap the finished platters or bowls in plastic to prevent spoiling and spills, and to discourage sampling by two- or four-legged taste testers. To keep the food from touching the wrap, erect a tent by inserting toothpicks in the corners and in the center of the food, then lay the plastic

To minimize kitchen duty, arrange food on serving dishes far in advance. The more time you have at the end, the less stressed you'll feel.

wrap on top of the toothpicks so it falls over the sides. If the plates' contents will dry out, as in the case of cut vegetables or sliced bread, cover them with slightly damp paper towels before you add the wrapping. Refrigerate as needed.

Always prepare more food than you anticipate will be needed. That way your table will look bountiful and inviting, and you'll ensure that even the hungriest guests can eat their fill without any guilt. Plus, you can avoid the host's classic

nightmare: running out of food. If you plan well, you'll have enough leftovers so you won't have to cook for a few days. To make the table look even more abundant, use small platters and pile up the sliced meats and cheeses, roasted vegetables, or cookies. Tip baskets on their sides so that rolls, fruit, or chips spill out of them. Place a base of shredded lettuce in the bottom of each bowl before filling it with pasta salad, marinated green beans, tapenade, or whole cherry tomatoes.

EASY GARNISHES

Garnishes. Maybe just hearing the word is enough to set your knees knocking. Never fear. Learning a few simple tricks can take the dread out of enhancing the presentation of your food.

A bounty of *textures, colors, and heights makes a dessert table look even more enticing. Leafy garnishes add a cooling counterpoint to the warm colors of baked goods.*

Beware of Poisonous Garnishes

Holly, calla lilies, and dandelion flowers are beautiful—and potentially fatal if eaten. When you use decorative greenery or flowers anywhere near food, be careful that they will not be ingested. Most plants are not poisonous, but it's better to check if you have doubts or questions. Call a nursery or a poison hot line (usually listed with emergency numbers in the front of the phone book).

The first items to reach for are fresh herbs. Be daring: You can go beyond the ubiquitous sprig of parsley, although chopped parsley sprinkled over the top of a tuna casserole is a delicious addition. Fresh herbs add color, aroma, and extra flavor.

grilled beef. Experiment. Once you start using fresh herbs, you'll taste the difference —and you'll wonder how you ever managed to get along without them.

Putting small decorative touches on food adds allure to your entire party, and need not consume much time or money. Here are a few ideas from the pros. To give soup bowls a festive look, mist the rims with cooking oil spray and sprinkle paprika around the edge. Line a small container with plastic wrap and fill it with a dip or spread, either homemade or store-bought. Let it sit in the fridge until it's firm, unmold it, and surround the bottom edge with edible flowers. If you have time to go a step farther, use a mold in the shape of a heart, a fish, a Christmas tree—anything that strikes your fancy or contributes to the mood. Brush egg whites onto miniature fruit or grape clusters, sprinkle them with granulated sugar, let dry, and use to trim a dessert or cheese platter. Drizzle colorful flavored oils (red pepper, lemon, or basil) on the edge of a platter of sliced

When guests' plates are empty, encourage them to help themselves to more. Set an example by serving yourself a second helping.

They make even the most ordinary bowl of rice look like a dish in a fine restaurant. There are few rules, a lot of room for improvisation—and almost no way to fail. For example, cilantro, either chopped or whole, is a natural for any Mexican food. Basil lends itself to almost anything Mediterranean, as does oregano, but don't chop these or they'll discolor. Whole sprigs of rosemary look beautiful around a plate of

meat, fish, or vegetables. Fill squeeze bottles with colored sauces and draw a decorative design on a plate.

You can also use fruits and vegetables to add color, texture, and height as well as to complement the dish itself. Combine whole red bell peppers with artichokes in the center of a platter. Surround a plate of pasta salad with bright red and yellow cherry tomatoes. Or use long strips of lemon peel to decorate a platter of salmon. Ingredients you've used in the food can often work well as garnishes too. Sprinkle curls and shavings of chocolate around a chocolate cake. Or surround a platter of enchiladas with whole chili peppers.

TABLE ETIQUETTE

Don't sit down and poise your knife and fork above your plate until you make sure that everyone else has a plate of food. If you have a buffet, serve yourself last. If you serve food from a bowl or platter, pass the items around the table or walk around with each platter and let guests serve themselves. If you have hired help to serve food at a sit-down meal, they should set a full plate down from the right and clear an empty plate from the left.

Now that everyone's seated, guests will look to you to start. If you want to begin the meal with a toast or other gesture, do so as soon as you sit down and all other guests are seated. You can also suggest that your company begin without you if you will be delayed. When guests' plates are empty, encourage them to help themselves to more, but don't force them. Set an example and begin by serving yourself a second helping.

Invariably a picky or restricted eater will attend your party. Fear not: You don't have to change your menu or cook a separate meal for just one person. The easiest solution is to plan in advance. Always build at least one nonmeat and nondairy dish into your menu. By using these two simple criteria, you can accommodate almost any dietary restriction.

Perk up your dishes *with simple garnishes. All it takes is a sprig of fresh basil or thyme or a few strips of lemon peel.*

If you don't have advance warning about a guest's dietary restrictions, and you learn about them as you sit down to eat, there are solutions. Ask what the guest can and will eat. Then check your menu to see if anything that is already prepared is acceptable. Usually there will be at least one food your guest will eat.

When the meal is coming to an end, you might encounter guests who want to smoke at the table. If others are still eating, ask the smokers to move to another room, or to smoke outside. Once dinner is over, anyone who wishes to smoke at the table may do so—after they've asked other guests whether they'd mind.

Remember that as host the most important role you play is that of leader. If you are enjoying yourself, others will too, regardless of any small difficulties.

CREATING the
PERFECT Bar

—✳—

1 Predinner **cocktails** are best limited to one hour; a cocktail party can last much longer. **2** For simplicity's sake, offer your guests the same **beverage selection** before, during, and after dinner. **3** Serve beverages you like and **feel comfortable** serving. Don't feel obliged to serve liquor if sodas and juice will do.

4 To **avoid surprises,** always have more food and beverages on hand than you think you'll need. **5** Decide which **finishing touches** are necessary. For martinis, olives are a must. Frilly toothpicks are not. **6** Offer a small **selection of snacks** that guests can pick up in one hand and eat in one bite. Nuts, olives, and chips are all **good choices.** **7** Master two or three drink recipes and **stock the ingredients** for impromptu gatherings.

8 Befriend your local wine merchant and ask for advice on the **right wines.** **9** Don't forget to stock up on plenty of **ice.** ●

POURING DRINKS WITH EASE

SIMPLE BEVERAGES AND SNACKS

——————*

Whether the occasion is cocktails for two, dinner for eight, or a fast and furious poker game, libations can set the mood. If wondering what to serve, how to serve it, and how much to buy leaves you feeling as shaken as a James Bond martini, relax. Life has enough stresses. Assembling a party bar doesn't have to be one of them.

To keep fuss to a minimum, serve only one beverage: your favorite, whether it's champagne, a pitcher of margaritas, or a selection of sodas. With very little effort you can go one step further and offer your guests their choice of wine. And don't worry if you're missing the kind of glass that's intended for a specific beverage. A one-style-fits-all wineglass is not only acceptable, it's chic. If you're starting to build a party closet, order one or two dozen inexpensive French bistro glasses from a kitchen-supply catalog and fill them with everything from apéritifs to orange juice.

COCKTAIL HOUR
AND BEYOND

B EFORE DINNER OR ON THEIR OWN, COCKTAILS ARE AN INSTITUTION. THE
PREMEAL COCKTAIL HOUR IS A GRACE PERIOD THAT ALLOWS GUESTS TO
ENJOY A LITTLE LAID-BACK CONVERSATION BEFORE THE MAIN EVENT BEGINS.

It's a time for everyone—including you—
to relax and cast off the stresses of the day.
Whether you're serving a meal at home
or whether you and your guests are heading off to a restaurant, try to limit cocktail
time to one hour. Otherwise, your guests
may become inebriated or famished before
dinner is set on the table.

Following the meal, no one really
expects after-dinner drinks, but they're

Location, Location, Location

The bar is often the busiest
place at your party, so where
you put it is as important as
what you put on it. The easiest
way to avoid traffic congestion,
especially at a large gathering,
is to set up two bars, perhaps
one on the dining-room table
and another one on the kitchen
counter. If that's not possible,
choose a spot that allows people
to approach the bar without
jostling one another.

a welcome, sophisticated treat. You can
close out the evening with a special touch
—at no effort whatsoever—if you keep a
bottle of Irish cream liqueur, cognac, port,
or ouzo on hand.

A self-contained cocktail party is an
early-evening get-together that typically
lasts two or three hours. Cocktail parties
give you a wonderful opportunity to entertain without having to provide a meal
(though you will probably want to offer
a range of snacks to your guests).

Of course, the starring attraction of
any cocktail party is the cocktail, so your
range of drinks calls for a bit of thought.
Don't try to guess what everyone's favorite
libation is; simply offer a selection of red
and white wine, beer, and soft drinks. If
you want to go a step further, add a single
mixed drink. Make it a basic, no-nonsense
drink, perhaps rum and cola or gin and
tonic—something that requires only a
few ingredients and no great expertise in
the secret art of mixology.

Whenever you're serving cocktails, lay
out a snack or two for your guests. Go with
easy finger foods such as chips and dip or
crackers and cheese. These offerings don't
need to be elaborate; a few bowls of mixed
roasted nuts will do just fine.

IDEAS FOR THE BAR

✳

CREATE A MEMORABLE BAR by using household objects in imaginative ways. Haul out apple barrels, wicker laundry baskets, and metal washtubs, and line them with plastic if you think they might leak. Make your most unusual and colorful glassware sparkle. You don't have to go overboard—just create a bar that's compatible with your lifestyle.

For outdoor parties, *a wheelbarrow makes an ideal cooler that can be moved easily. Just fill with ice, load with bottles and cans of your favorite drinks, and roll to the perfect location.*

For a tropical theme *party, dress up an ordinary tin bucket with ti leaves or palm fronds. Hold the leaves in place with raffia or twine.*

For simplicity's sake, *limit your bar to one or two choices—perhaps a festive bucketful of sparkling and white wines.*

Offer your guests *pitchers of luscious infused spirits made with fresh berries or citrus fruits marinated in vodka or tequila.*

Beverage Selection and Inventory

I T'S EASY TO CHOOSE A DRINK FOR YOURSELF: ORDER WHAT YOU LIKE. SET THE SAME STANDARDS WHEN ENTERTAINING BY SERVING YOUR GUESTS WHAT YOU PREFER TO DRINK. LET YOUR OWN TASTE AND COMFORT LEVEL BE YOUR GUIDE.

If you never imbibe anything stronger than wine or beer, make that the limit of your inventory. If you're an expert at mixing Manhattans, go for it.

Aim to please a broad audience. When you're entertaining a mixed-drinks crowd, you can't go wrong with the basics: Scotch, bourbon, rum, vodka, gin, and tequila. Just include a stock of traditional mixers (water, soda, tonic), some lemon and lime wedges, swizzle sticks, and a few buckets of ice. A "perfect bar" isn't just about alcohol. Always include sodas, bottled water, and fruit juices for designated drivers and others who socialize without imbibing.

To be more creative but still keep it simple, buy an assortment of apéritifs and serve them over ice. If you have a friend who prides himself on making the best martinis

What beverage goes with what food? Forget experts' ideas about correct pairings. Serve whatever combination pleases you.

in town, press him into service. Or host a "Bring Your Own Booze" happy hour and ask your friends to come with their own choice of favorite libations.

Let your favorite drink become the inspiration behind your party.

THE NO-CHOICE BAR

TO KEEP THE PARTY SIMPLE, serve only one type of beverage at your gathering. Tell guests in advance that they're invited for something like a white-wine sampling, a tequila fiesta with tortilla chips and salsa, or an array of fresh-fruit smoothies.

Simple

Offer a range of one type of liquor. If you and your friends are Scotch lovers, for example, stock your bar with a few kinds of highland and lowland single malts.

Simpler

Have a serve-yourself bar. Pick a single spirit such as vodka and enhance it by offering a range of mixers, so that martini drinkers and vodka-tonic lovers alike can help themselves.

Simplest

You can't go wrong by serving the classiest of all beverages: champagne. It makes a welcome change from non-bubbly wines and beer. Serve sparkling cider to guests who don't imbibe.

Even when you are offering several drink choices, serving needn't be a big production. Forget the idea of a classic bar. For a really informal get-together, leave beer, white wine, and soft drinks in the fridge; put red wine, liquor, and glasses on the kitchen counter and let your guests help themselves. If your kitchen space is too cramped for guests to maneuver comfortably, commandeer a table in the living room. Simply cover it with an attractive cloth and set out your supplies: liquor and mixers, glasses, bar tools, towels, and buckets of ice. Extras can stay in the refrigerator until you need them.

FOOD PAIRINGS

How do you tackle the classic dilemma: deciding what beverage goes with what food? The simple answer—don't. Forget the experts' ideas about correct pairings of food and drink. Just serve whatever combination pleases you. If you like gin and tonic with your flank steak, prefer Chardonnay with your spaghetti, or love Chianti with your Dover sole, serve that to guests. If champagne is your idea of the all-purpose beverage and you drink it with everything from lasagna to chocolate-chip cookies, remember that the culinary cops are not going to knock at your door and whisk the crystal flutes from your table: The process of pairing a beverage with a particular dish is highly subjective.

There are, however, some historical guidelines and some culinary traditions you can rely on for inspiration if you're determined to follow the rules of more traditional pairings. Just remember that white wine goes well with pale-colored foods and red wine complements dark-colored foods. If you happen to like a particular wine or have a more adventurous palate, reverse the rule occasionally to

Simply Put...

ALCOHOLIC DRINKS

apéritif • Any alcoholic drink (be it beer, wine, or mixed drink) that's served before lunch or dinner to welcome guests and whet the appetite.

digestif • A spirit served after a meal; brandy or grappa, for example.

liqueur • Often called a cordial, this syrupy beverage typically gets its strong, sweet flavor from the essence of a plant, seed, or fruit. Serve after a meal. Includes schnapps and ouzo.

spirits • Strong alcoholic beverages made by distillation. Scotch, bourbon, gin, rum, and vodka are examples of spirits. Wine, hard cider, and beer, which are fermented, are not.

discover new combinations that appeal to you—Merlot with salmon, or Sauvignon Blanc with beef-and-broccoli stir-fry.

Contemporary matches can often be created by pairing the specific characteristics of a food with a beverage that enhances them. It's not as intimidating as it may seem. All types of food can be divided into four taste categories: sweet, sour, salty, and spicy. The best taste combinations complement each other. If you decide to serve spicy Mexican or Asian foods, pour a slightly sweet wine such as Gewürztraminer or a lager or amber ale. Sour food, which can include anything high in acid, such as tomato sauce or vinaigrette dressing, calls for a more robust beverage, like

a full-bodied red wine. Anything goes with salty food—it tastes great paired with all kinds of beverages. If your menu encompasses a variety of taste categories but you want to stick to one beverage, choose one that will complement the most prominent dish. For desserts, choose wines that are on the sweet side, or offer classic after-dinner drinks such as port or cognac.

Alternatively, let your guests choose which beverage they want to drink with their food. Provide two to three different cocktails that all go well with your hors d'oeuvres. During the meal you offer red wine, white wine, or both, and let guests pick the combination they like the best. Whatever you choose to serve to your guests, just make sure that you have a plentiful supply of beverages on hand.

STOCKING UP

A well-stocked liquor cabinet is a luxury, not a necessity. What's better by far is to have a well-*selected* bar—one that's ready with the things you and your friends drink on a regular basis, rather than one that takes too much of your time and money. And remember, distilled spirits do not go bad, nor is it likely that the bottles you buy will be emptied at a single gathering. Think of the bar you assemble now as an investment in future entertaining.

In addition to the liquor and mixers you choose, plan to buy white and red wines. Serve white wines chilled (though not icy cold) and reds at room temperature. If wine shopping strikes you as a time-consuming and expensive process, don't worry. Quite often you can find excellent, inexpensive wines as close as your supermarket or local liquor store, which will sometimes offer good buys.

HOW MUCH TO BUY?

Deciding how much of everything you're going to need for a gathering might seem like sheer guesswork, but it's not. There's a basic formula. To ensure that you're not caught short, err on the generous side and assume that each of your guests will quaff two drinks per hour. A standard-size bottle of wine or champagne (750ml) yields five or six servings. The same-size bottle of spirits provides about 17 drinks if you pour a one-and-a-half-ounce (45ml) shot. And a 12-ounce (355ml) can of beer serves one. As with all party consumables, you'll avoid unwanted surprises if you buy more than you think you'll need.

Possibly the most crucial key to a stress-free party is plenty of ice. Whether you use ice in individual drinks or in a big tub to chill bottles, running out of it can be trouble. Always fill buckets and coolers to their capacity, and figure that each guest will consume at least a quarter to a half pound (125–250g) of cubes.

For a smooth-running party, stock up on glasses. Buy, rent, or borrow them, but make sure you have more than you think you'll need. To keep things simple, especially if you're hosting a large gathering, rely on one all-purpose glass. A 10- or 12-ounce (300 or 355ml) size will handle all beverages with ease. If you're a stickler for details or if you want to start building a collection, shop for these classic shapes: highball, old-fashioned, red wine, white

Varied sizes and types *of glasses make for a striking presentation. You can often find beautiful stemware or colored glassware in antique shops and secondhand stores.*

wine, champagne, martini, and margarita. They needn't all match. An eclectic collection of classic crystal, quirky thrift-store finds, and handblown creations from your favorite craftsperson makes a great conversation starter. Don't let propriety fence you

Chill a Bottle Quickly

When the impulse to entertain moves you, and you need to chill a bottle or a six-pack in a hurry, here's a quick solution. Fill a bucket or high-sided container with ice. Then add enough water so that when the bottle or cans are submerged, the water climbs at least halfway up the sides of the beverage containers.

Your local wine merchant is a rich source
of information just waiting to be tapped.

in. It's perfectly OK to use plastic, especially for large and boisterous gatherings, outdoor parties, or occasions when young children are set free to romp.

Shopping for bar accessories is fun—and you don't have to spend a bundle.

How Many Glasses per Person?

Guests often set their glasses down and then forget which one is theirs. Be prepared and stock more glasses than you think you'll need. To ensure that you won't run out, stock at least one glass per person per hour. It never hurts to have more—who wants to wash glasses in the middle of a party?

Keep a sharp eye out for intriguing and practical items you can find in houseware and kitchen stores, antique and thrift shops, and mail-order catalogs. Here are the basic accessories you'll need:

◆ A GOOD CORKSCREW AND A COUPLE OF BOTTLE OPENERS (WITH POINTED ENDS FOR OPENING CANS OF JUICE)

◆ A LONG-HANDLED SPOON FOR MIXING DRINKS IN PITCHERS, AND SWIZZLE STICKS FOR INDIVIDUAL GLASSES

◆ A SHOT GLASS OR JIGGER SO YOU CAN MEASURE PRECISE AMOUNTS FOR MIXED COCKTAILS

◆ A SMALL CUTTING BOARD AND PARING KNIFE TO SLICE LEMONS AND LIMES

◆ COCKTAIL NAPKINS—PAPER IS EASIEST

Everything else is probably already in your kitchen, including a blender for specialty drinks such as frozen margaritas, daiquiris, or piña coladas, and clean dish towels or cloth napkins to mop up spills and catch the overflow from effervescent beverages.

To simplify your beverage shopping, divide your list into three categories: spirits, which may outlast more than one festive occasion; wine and beer, which you'll serve more often; and mixers and soft drinks, which will come in handy any time you have guests.

It pays to invest in good wine and spirits. Build your inventory over time and store it well. A cool, dark cupboard can house everything you keep on hand: tightly sealed liquor bottles, wine bottles on their sides, and unopened mixers.

Liquor may well be the most expensive ingredient of your party (and it pays to buy the best that your budget allows), but you can assemble a fine bar without spending a fortune. Be on the lookout for sales; explore discount outlets and warehouse stores; ask friends, store clerks, and bartenders to recommend quality brands at less-than-premium prices. But beware of the bottle bearing a price tag that's too good to be true: Once you taste it, you'll probably find it's not such a bargain.

When shopping time comes, it's easy to end up feeling overwhelmed. How do you choose among the hundreds of various beers, wines, and spirits lining store shelves? You can always stick to the same couple of brands you've served for years, or simply ask the clerk for suggestions.

If you'd like to branch out and experiment now and then, ask a staff member at your local liquor store for suggestions and descriptions of their best sellers. When you go out to dinner, ask the sommelier or a knowledgeable waiter to recommend the type of wine that will best complement the food you've ordered.

You don't have to become an expert, but doing some homework will make the

Liquor Rationing

When spirits are to be mixed with other ingredients, their flavor quality is not as important as when they are to be served straight. Feel free to purchase lesser-quality brands when you'll be serving mixed drinks, and save the pricey brands for the times you're serving spirits on the rocks.

selection process easier (besides, it's fun). Read the wine and spirits sections of your local newspaper and glossy food magazines. Drop into a wine shop and browse through the shelves. Most of these shops have periodic tasting sessions; you can go to a few and take notes on the varieties you like. Or find out from friends what brands of various beverages they prefer. Remember one word of caution, however: Always try a beverage yourself before you decide to serve it to guests.

BOTTLED GIFTS

After you have selected your beverages, you're bound to get some surprises: One or two of your guests will undoubtedly present you with a bottle as they walk through the door. If the gift enhances the drink selection, go ahead and open it. If you already have plenty of opened bottles or this one just doesn't fit the occasion or your drink menu, save it to be enjoyed later. Your guests will understand.

Snacks and Drinks

Nothing could be simpler to prepare than good bar snacks. In fact, some of the best ones require no preparation at all: Simply pour them into a bowl and you're ready to greet your guests.

Ideally, these nibbles should be things you can pick up with one hand and pop into your mouth. You can't go wrong with a few bowls of potato chips, nuts, and pretzels. They'll keep your guests happy until dinner—and they'll provide a cushion to stave off the effects of the alcohol.

You can make party snacks look much grander than they are by presenting them in unexpected ways. Instead of setting out big bowls of nuts or olives, for instance, divide them among a few colorful bowls, decorative glass containers, or small baskets lined with napkins. Or arrange individual servings of crackers, nuts, chips, and pretzels on small plates and set them out next to chairs, couches, and benches.

Don't worry about serving a meal's worth of appetizers. Your guests know this is meant to be nibble food, not dinner. Figure that each adult will consume one or two handfuls of nuts or chips, and two to four individual servings of finger food

Avoid putting snacks on the bar. That's where everyone congregates, and if guests find food there, they'll never leave.

per hour. Nevertheless, it's a good idea to be prepared for big eaters by keeping a backup supply of snacks on hand.

If you've not serving dinner after the cocktails, you can treat guests to a few hors d'oeuvres that are more sophisticated and substantial. Buy cooked prawns and serve them with a bowl or two of prepared

Make snacks accessible
to every guest.

ONE TOO MANY

THERE'S NO DOUBT ABOUT IT—alcohol can liven up a social gathering. But a common and important concern among hosts is how to discourage guests from overindulging and then getting behind the wheel. There are a few techniques for avoiding trouble.

Simple Serve plenty of food at parties where people are drinking alcohol, and always have a nonalcoholic specialty drink or beverage ready to offer designated drivers.

Simpler Select a cutoff time for serving alcohol. At the appointed time, begin serving only nonalcoholic beverages and coffee. Then put away the alcohol so guests will not be tempted.

Simplest If it's time for everyone to leave and you have a guest who has drunk too much, call a cab or offer a place to sleep. It's much better than letting the guest drive while intoxicated.

sauce for dipping. Or wrap gourmet bread-sticks with prosciutto and arrange them attractively on a plate.

When you plan which snacks to serve at your party, try to avoid anything messy that your guests are likely to spill on themselves or on your furniture. And always have lots of cocktail napkins around for wiping hands, wrapping around glasses, and cleaning up minor spills.

At a large party, place snacks around the room so every guest has easy access. For a small party, set them on a coffee table or other center of attraction. Avoid putting snacks on the bar. That's where everyone congregates, and if guests find food there, they'll never leave.

MIXOLOGY DEMYSTIFIED

At a cocktail party, the emphasis is on the contents of your guests' glasses. You can hire a bartender (see page 59 for tips on hiring one), or set out a selection of bottles and let guests mix their own drinks. What if you want to play bartender and mix drinks yourself? Don't panic. You need not master a dozen complicated drink recipes; just learn one or two very well, and your guests will be pleased.

The next time you visit your preferred watering hole, watch the bartender whip up your favorite libation. Study his or her technique, write down the ingredients, and if there's something you don't understand, ask questions. Then go home and replicate what you've learned. Practice concocting your drinks a few times before you serve them to friends. Once you've become a whiz at mixing a dry martini or making Irish coffee, or you can honestly say your own Cosmopolitan is as good as any you've tasted in a bar (and it won't take long), you'll have the beginnings of your cocktail-party repertoire.

ADD **Atmosphere**

with **SIMPLE STEPS**

1 Greet your guests by placing **seasonal props** such as pine-cones, pumpkins, or sunflowers on your front porch. **2** Buy or **decorate a cake** to match the occasion—for example, a ship for a bon-voyage party. **3** Guests themselves can become decorations when you festoon them with **Mardi Gras** beads, cowboy hats for a barbecue, or leis for a Hawaiian luau. **4** Start your decorations search at home. **Ransack your closets** and cupboards. Wicker baskets can be filled with paper plates, napkins, and utensils for an out-door buffet. **5** **Create ambience** by filling your home with candles, soft music, and flowers. **6** Add fragrance to your party by **dabbing aromatic oil** on light bulbs or filling a room with scented candles. **7** If you don't have enough seating, **use throw pillows** on the floor; bring outdoor furniture inside or vice versa. **8** **Greet guests** as they arrive and introduce each person to at least one other guest. **9** Treat your guests to a slide show, a board game, **a scavenger hunt,** or a few card games. ●

SETTING
the STAGE

WAYS TO MAKE YOUR PARTY MEMORABLE

——————*

You've planned the party, invited guests, chosen the menu, cooked the food, stocked the bar, and lined up help. But instead of patting yourself on the back, you panic. Your mind launches into a monologue: "I should have changed the drapes, replaced the rugs, cleaned out the gutters"—on and on you'll go as a result of last-minute jitters.

Relax. Remember, your guests are coming to spend time with you, not to assess your interior-decorating talent or to count the dust bunnies under the beds. The hardest part of entertaining is behind you. All you have to do now is fly through a room or two with a vacuum cleaner and put out the welcome mat. If you want to light a few candles, arrange some flowers in vases, put on some music, or even decorate your house from garage to attic—and you have the time— you can do it with a minimum of fuss. But don't bother with any of this unless it's what you really want to do.

Preparing the Site

UNLESS YOU HAVE HELP, EITHER HIRED OR VOLUNTARY, DON'T EVEN TRY TO CLEAN YOUR HOUSE FROM TOP TO BOTTOM. YOUR GUESTS AREN'T GOING TO PASS JUDGMENT ON YOUR HOUSEKEEPING.

And chances are your guests will see only a few rooms anyway. Give those rooms a quick once-over and let it go at that.

If you have time to clean only a single room, make it the bathroom. Most people can overlook a little dirt almost anywhere else, but this room—at least the sink and toilet—should be spotless. A few quick swipes with some spray cleaner and a brush will do the job in minutes. Then hang up clean towels, toss clutter—your toiletries and terry robe, the kids' rubber ducks and sailboats—into the bathtub, and close the shower curtain or door. Sweep the floor.

Move on to the part of the house your guests will see first: the entry and hallway. Here people get their first impression of your home, but making that impression

a favorable one can be as simple as clearing out the clutter—stray coats, toys, old mail. Don't worry about getting everything to its proper home; just stash it out of sight and deal with it later.

TACKLING PARTY ROOMS

Next, sort out the rooms where guests will spend most of their time—most likely the living and dining rooms. First, declutter the living room. If you have time to get the newspapers to the recycling bin, the kids' toys to their bedroom shelves, the sweaters to their rightful owners, all the better. If not, just gather everything up and stow it in a closet or out-of-the-way bedroom.

Then give the place a quick once-over with a vacuum cleaner and a lint-free rag. Don't bother washing the windows or the glass on picture frames. Don't feel that you have to mop the floor or clean the carpet (they'll only be dirty again in a few hours). If you want to do more because your mother's coming to the party, spritz any spots with a spray cleaner made for carpet, wood, or tile.

Even if you're having a sit-down dinner party, it's a snap to make the dining room presentable. All you have to do is vacuum the floor, then wipe the table and sideboard with spray cleaner or furniture polish. If the tabletop still flaunts its nicks

Quick Fixes for Worn Furniture

Buy one-size-fits-all slipcovers for the sofas and chairs. (Make sure they're washable.) Cover less-than-gorgeous tables with a colorful tablecloth or blanket. Use geegaws to hide small holes or dents in your furniture.

Last-minute cleaning shortcuts are all you need before a party.

and gouges (and you view them as flaws, not marks of character), drape it with one of your favorite tablecloths.

Your bedroom may be moonlighting as a catchall for coats and handbags. It deserves some attention, but a few minutes' worth will be plenty. Just put away items you don't want guests to see, then smooth out the wrinkles in the bedspread.

PREPARING THE KITCHEN

Giving the kitchen a last-minute cleaning can be tricky. Not to worry; this too can be handled with some planning and a little sleight of hand. If you leave everything until the very end, the job will seem insurmountable. Instead, clean as you go along. As soon as you finish using a dish, wash it, dry it, and put it away, or load it in the dishwasher. Then, as the minutes tick by until the first buzz of the doorbell, all you will have to do is clear the area of items you won't be using for the party, and then

wipe down the counters, cabinet doors, refrigerator front, and stove top with a spray cleaner and some paper towels.

EDITING CONTENTS

Finally, make a pass through all the rooms that guests will be using and quickly edit the contents. Remove extraneous furniture such as small tables too wobbly to hold drinks, or pretty but uncomfortable chairs no one ever sits in. If you own anything so precious that its destruction would ruin your evening (or your life), lock it up.

As party time nears, it's easy to get caught up in a cleaning frenzy. You may wish that you'd hired a cleaning service, but you can still make your home look as attractive as possible in the time available. Don't go overboard. Put yourself in your guests' place: Would you rather spend several hours with a host who's worn out, or one who's relaxed, energetic, and having as enjoyable a time as you are?

HOW TO DECORATE

---✳---

DECORATING IS LIKE ICING ON A CAKE: IT ISN'T REALLY NECESSARY, BUT IT SURE IS SWEET. PARTY DECORATIONS CAN COMMUNICATE A THEME, COMMEMORATE AN OCCASION, CELEBRATE A SEASON, OR EXPRESS A MOOD.

There's only one hard-and-fast rule: Have fun when you decorate. If it's not enjoyable or it strikes you as a chore, forget it.

For most people, the stressful part of decorating isn't finding or arranging the trimmings; it's deciding what to use in the first place. There's a simple way you can kick-start the process. Ask yourself what you want the party's surroundings to communicate. Are you decorating to carry out a particular party theme or to honor a special occasion? Do you want to project

Seasonal decor *is usually simple to find. Celebrate the harvest or Thanksgiving with cornstalks, bales of hay, and pumpkins.*

a holiday mood or one of glamour, fun, or whimsy? Or do you simply want to present your guests with an atmosphere in which they will be comfortable and relaxed?

If you can think of some objects that will help convey your intentions, make note of them. For an Easter lunch, you might try stuffed bunnies and chocolate eggs. Maybe you have a collection of old wooden toys that projects a whimsical feeling. Making a place homey and relaxing is as easy as lighting candles and lining the mantel with fresh-smelling greenery.

Next, think about the location. Which parts of your home or the event site do you want to disguise or showcase? Bear in mind that the front porch is among the easiest areas to decorate. So are ceilings, windows, walls, and horizontal surfaces such as mantels and tabletops. Once you've decided where you want to put your decorations, decide how many items you'll need and how big the arrangement should be.

MAKING A STATEMENT

People milling around a room with glasses in their hands could mean anything. Decorations announce loudly and clearly what your party is about. Put a Christmas tree in the corner, and any passerby will know exactly what's going on. Seasonal parties are the easiest of all to decorate for because their symbols have been part of our lives since earliest childhood. And those seasonal symbols have the added advantage of being easy to come by. What could be simpler than honoring the autumn harvest with an apple-filled bucket flanking the front door? To carry the theme inside the house, tie stalks of dried wheat onto the backs of dining chairs; fill baskets with squash, dried red chilies, and decorative gourds, and set them on tables.

Pay homage to winter by stringing paper snowflakes from the ceiling with clear fishing line and tape. (Your children will be happy to cut out the snowflakes, or recruit a neighbor's kids.) Use a rustic sled as a centerpiece on a buffet table. Line your fireplace mantel with greens and citrus. Fasten a crossed pair of snow skis together and hang them above your doorway.

Later in the year, help everyone shed the cold-weather blues and emerge from hibernation by staging an ode to spring. Create a paradise with blooming tulips, hyacinths, and freesias in large containers. Buy flats of wheat grass and build a little lawn down the center of your table. Fill vases with fresh asparagus spears.

PUTTING IDEAS IN PLACE

Say you want to have people over, but you're still not clear on how to establish a theme and reinforce it with decorations. The following ideas might provide you with some inspiration.

Invite friends for a video marathon, and hang a movie poster on the front door. Serve dinner in compartmentalized plates on TV trays, then pass around dessert: a

Centerpiece Height

Large arrangements of flowers or objets d'art are captivating—unless they obstruct the view between you and the person across the table. Keep center-pieces under 12 inches (30cm).

bowl filled with boxes of "movie" candy. For decorations now and snacks later, fill small brown paper bags with popcorn and line them up along the mantel.

Throw an indoor garden party, using birdhouses as centerpieces. Place a watering can next to gardening gloves, hand tools, a sun hat, and packets of seeds.

Ask yourself what you want the party surroundings to communicate. Then make a list of objects that will convey your intentions.

Make a baby shower even more special by decorating with items the expectant parents can take home. Pile gifts in a stroller or bassinet. Fill a baby's bathtub with small bath toys and animal-shaped sponges. Use baby bottles as vases. Make a garland of teething toys and pacifiers tied onto colorful ribbons.

Add a touch of romance to a wedding anniversary party by drawing a heart on the bathroom mirror with a red lipstick to frame your guests' faces. Sprinkle dime-store gold and silver rings across a table.

Create a poster from an original wedding photo of the honored couple and add congratulatory messages from all the guests.

Send off a traveling friend with a bon-voyage party. Use maps as place mats or a tablecloth. Line up suitcases across the front porch. Stock the bar with miniature bottles of liquor like those served on airplanes. Cover serving trays with postcards.

KEEPING IT EASY

Once you have chosen a theme, remember that decorations can be simple or elaborate, subtle or bold, homemade or store bought. They can be priceless antiques or junk rescued from the sidewalk. The simplest approach is to visit your local party-supply store and buy decorations appropriate to the occasion.

Apart from that, one of the easiest and most clever ways to decorate is to use ordinary objects in intriguing new ways. Group some antique toys in the middle of a table, and voilà—a centerpiece. Arrange a bunch of flowers in an old teapot, and you've got a new vase. Haul out your collection of egg cups and turn them into delightful holders for votive candles.

For truly effortless decorating, think food. After all, you're already planning to feed people; you might as well turn your menu into decor. Buy a cake decorated to match the occasion, such as a sailboat or airplane for a bon-voyage party. For a Christmas party, prepare food using ingredients such as green bell peppers and red tomato sauces for pasta. Cut biscuits into heart shapes and spread them with strawberry jam for a Valentine's Day brunch.

Guests themselves can become party decorations. Pass out colorful Mardi Gras beads and feather masks to get the revelry

LASTING IMPRESSIONS

❋

IT'S OFTEN THE SMALL TOUCHES that your guests remember best: the table setting, the flowers, the unique conversation piece. Perhaps you've never tried these types of decorative effects before. All are easy to create with little effort or expense. In fact, you may already have many of these items on hand at home.

Roll a cloth or paper *napkin into a cylinder and fasten it with a piece of kitchen twine. Tuck in a few sprigs of rosemary or lavender.*

Create a centerpiece *that symbolizes abundance or the harvest. Fill a galvanized box or pail with fresh fruits and berries.*

Float candles *and gardenias in a large glass bowl for a fragrant and dramatic display.*

Transform empty *mineral water, wine, olive oil, and other colored glass bottles into vases. Assemble them in clusters and place single-stemmed flowers, such as cosmos, in each.*

rolling on Fat Tuesday. Deck party goers with leis for a Hawaiian luau, cowboy hats and lassos for a Western theme, mood rings for a seventies nostalgia night, or sombreros for a Cinco de Mayo fiesta.

FINDING MATERIALS

Small details can often cause the most headaches. Who has time to race all over town looking for just the right decorative touches? There's no need to venture far. With a little imagination and ingenuity, you'll find everything you need close at hand: in your home, your garage, or neighborhood stores.

Start your search at home. Ransack your closets, cupboards, and attic. Shiny glass Christmas tree ornaments gathered in a silver bowl become a timeless holiday centerpiece. Empty your wicker baskets of those never-to-be-read magazines, and fill them up with paper plates, napkins, and utensils for an outdoor buffet.

Clean out your garage. An aging Red Flyer wagon filled with ice becomes the perfect cooler chest for bottled beers. Dust off a wreath from the attic, place a large candle in the middle, and use it as a centerpiece for the table or buffet.

Shop local stores. Terra-cotta, ceramic, or galvanized containers—all of which are readily found at hardware stores and nurseries—lend a decorative touch when brimming with flowers, fruit, or squash. An inexpensive full-length mirror—laid on top of your buffet table—becomes a dramatic surface for serving all manner of party food. Surround the large mirror with smaller ones, and hide any unsightly edges with greens and flowering vines.

Simple entertaining means making creative use of what is readily available. Once you've poked into the attic and all the closets in your house, you'll come up with plenty of treasures to use as decorations for your celebration.

Decorating for the holidays is easy. Christmas offers lots of opportunities to dress up your home—and yourself.

CREATING AMBIENCE

———— ✳ ————

Have you ever been to a party or dinner where everything was perfect—the room felt comfortable, the mood was just right, and the company seemed to meld like long-lost friends?

That perfection was ambience: a distinctive atmosphere that surrounds a person, a location, or an object. You can think of it as invisible decor. It's a suggestion rather than an order; a hint, not a declaration. The ambience of your party will surround your guests with sights, smells, and sounds —and you can achieve it without putting up a single decoration.

Whether you're hosting a romantic interlude or a rambunctious get-together, a formal commemoration or a casual festivity, you can create an atmosphere to match. Ambience is easy to achieve without any fuss. For starters, break down the main elements of ambience—essentially scent, lighting, music, and crowd control —and add a small dose of each to make your party a raving success.

THE LURE OF SCENTS

Scents are the most powerful emotional stimulants of all. Just a whiff of freshly cut grass or the distinctive aroma of an apple pie baking in the oven can launch a flood of childhood memories. When it comes to building ambience at party time or anytime, scents are indispensable tools.

One of the easiest ways to add scent to your party is to dab aromatic oil on light bulbs. You can find dozens of aromatic oils in health-food stores, but it's simpler to use your favorite perfume or scented bath oil. Another way to fill the air with both fragrance and romantic light is to place aromatic candles around the room. The fragrances range from vanilla to pine, but always sample them before your guests arrive. The scent can sometimes be too strong and not always what you'd expect from the description. Besides, you don't want it to overpower or conflict with other scents, such as that of your cuisine.

One of the most inviting aromas— and among the easiest to produce—is that of cooking. Even if you're not serving dinner to your guests, a few simple tricks will

Burning Time of Candles

Depending on the length and width of a candle, its burning time can vary from one hour to several hours. Check the bottom of the package to find out. If you prefer not to be relighting candles during your party, start with new candles, or use long-lasting wide pillars instead of votives or tapers.

send the perfume of a season wafting through the room. To evoke a winter-holiday mood, fill a pot with water; add cinnamon sticks, whole cloves, or both, and let the mixture simmer on the stove. Or buy a prepared mixture. For a more savory aroma, spread whole sprigs of fresh rosemary on a baking sheet and set it in the oven turned to its lowest setting.

In a fireplace, enhance the perfume of burning wood by adding fresh herb stalks. For a classic token of welcome, as very little effort. For example, you could string tiny white Christmas lights through a tree's branches (indoors or outside). Use small lamps with flexible necks to back-light flower arrangements or to spotlight table displays. Position upward-pointing lights on the floor so that they shine up through the foliage of large houseplants.

Candlelight is a welcome addition to any party. Cluster candles of varying shapes, textures, and heights. Use them everywhere. Group votives on tabletops

For the most flattering light of all, use pink or peach-toned lightbulbs; they give everyone a healthy glow.

well as an aid to relaxation, soak lavender stalks (fresh or dried) in water for 10 to 15 minutes, then set them on top of the fire. To add enticing scent to a barbecue, toss in a few stalks of fresh rosemary.

MOOD LIGHTING

There's no doubt about it: Lighting makes a big impact on the mood of your party. Fortunately, it doesn't take a degree in interior design to create a scene that makes your guests look good and feel relaxed. In fact, it can be as simple as turning off the overhead lights and putting low-watt (60 or under) bulbs in all the lamps. For the most flattering light of all, use pink or peach-toned bulbs (available at larger hardware stores); they give everyone in the room a healthy-looking glow. Add a generous mix of candles, and you'll have a room no one will want to leave.

If you want to go a bit further, you can create dramatic lighting effects with and line them up along the windowsills and bookshelves. Populate the mantel with taper-filled candlesticks. Float candles in galvanized buckets, even in the bathtub. Scatter hurricane lamps with pillar candles inside them around the deck, and flank the sidewalk with lines of luminarias. In summer, add a liberal sprinkling of citronella candles to help repel insects.

Beyond lighting candles and stringing lights in the backyard, there are several other methods of casting illumination on your party scene that are simple to pull off. For a nautical theme, look for galvanized or other metal lanterns that burn candles or oil. Place them on a table, or hang them from the corners of the house. Create an island theme with a few bamboo tiki torches. These are easy to find in the garden section of large household stores and hardware stores. Insert them directly into the ground, or secure them in large plant containers.

AMBIENCE ENHANCERS

✳

THE RIGHT PARTY ATMOSPHERE can relax guests in moments. It takes just a bit of time to create an inviting place with pleasant fragrances, soft lighting, music, and favorite possessions. Consider purchasing some three-way lamps or dimmer switches if you entertain regularly. Both let you adjust your lighting to suit the occasion.

Showcase that old turntable *you've stashed in the garage and play those old records you've always loved.*

Luminarias *lead guests to the front door. Put votives in paper bags weighted with rice or sand.*

Add soft illumination *to a wall with this theatrical effect. Place uplights behind large plants and other decorative objects.*

Use the power *of scent to draw your guests into a room and create a mood. Fill a large pot of water with citrus and spices, and let it simmer.*

Turn off the overhead lights and use candles to help guests feel relaxed.

SAYING IT WITH MUSIC

Music has the power to invigorate, relax, inspire—or set teeth on edge. It can fade softly into the background, or it can be the star attraction of the gathering. But if you really can't tell a sonata from a ballad —and don't care to—you can dispense with music altogether. Chances are no one will really notice its absence.

The simplest way to add music to your gathering is to invest in a few CDs with appropriate tunes. To put people at ease and set a relaxed tone, you can't go wrong with mellow jazz or classical; for a boisterous party, opt for samba, rock-and-roll, jazz, or Dixie music.

No matter what type of music you choose to play, volume control is essential. Set it high enough so that everyone can hear the music, but low enough so they can still hear each other. If you plan to play loud music for dancing, alert the neighbors in advance—and even then don't blast it; assume that no one outside the room wants to hear it.

No pile of CDs can match the magic of live music. If you possibly can, hire a musician for the evening or ask a talented friend to perform. Connect the music to the party's theme, or vice versa. Match a calypso band to a taste-of-the-Caribbean gathering. Enlist a student opera singer to evoke a night in Italy. Hire a folksinger or guitarist to add authentic down-home flavor to a backyard barbecue.

THE COMFORT FACTOR

Beyond good food, plenty of drink, and adequate rest-room facilities, party goers need three things: room to move around, places to sit, and surfaces on which to set food and drinks. Luckily, you can provide all three with little fuss. For an intimate gathering, simply arrange your chairs and sofas around a low central table laden with food and drink. A larger group requires more planning, but don't let that intimidate you. A few simple steps are really all it takes. First, create the space to accommodate everyone on your guest list. Move

you'll probably use them often anyway. Arrange the seats in groups of three and four to facilitate easy conversation. If you're serving a buffet, make sure there's ample surface area—whether it's the floor, tabletop, or counter—for guests to set

If you don't have seats for everyone, haul in some outdoor furniture (or vice versa if it's an outdoor gathering).

small tables and other pieces of furniture out of the center of the living room and out of the hallway and the kitchen.

Then take stock of all your available seating: chairs, sofas, and benches. If you don't have enough seats for everyone, haul in some outdoor furniture (or vice versa if it's an outdoor gathering). Rent chairs or borrow a few from neighbors, or toss large throw pillows on the floor. If you don't have enough pillows, buy a few;

down their food and drink. Next, clear some paths to and around the buffet, to the bathroom, and to the back door and yard, where people may gather to smoke or for a breath of fresh air.

Making your guests feel comfortable isn't complicated or mysterious. When you're in doubt, just think about all the things that make you feel cozy, relaxed, and festive, and make sure that there's an abundance of these to go around.

SIMPLE SOLUTIONS

CONTINUOUS MUSIC

ONCE YOU'VE DECIDED WHAT TYPE of music to play, make sure it lasts the length of your party. There are several ways to do this without having to stand next to the stereo all night. And if you do need to tend to some music changes, ask a guest to help.

Simple Hire a band or disc jockey to play your favorite tunes. Discuss the length of the party and how many breaks they will take. Ask if they can play filler music during their breaks to avoid dead air.

Simpler Select CDs or mix cassette tapes to play throughout the party. If your system only holds one CD at a time, borrow a multi-CD unit from a friend so you don't need to attend to it constantly.

Simplest Find a radio station that plays music matching the mood of your party. Turn the radio on beforehand to make sure that the music hasn't been preempted by sports or talk programs.

ADJUSTING THE PACE

---- ✳ ----

THE BEST WAY TO WELCOME GUESTS TO YOUR HOME IS ALSO THE SIMPLEST: UNLESS IT'S ABSOLUTELY IMPOSSIBLE, PERSONALLY GREET EACH GUEST AT THE DOOR WITH A BIG SMILE AND A HUG, A KISS, OR A HANDSHAKE.

If you must leave the door, ask a friend or relative to stand in for a few minutes. Use a closet or bedroom to stash your guests' coats, purses, and scarves. (This is a great opportunity to get the kids involved; have them help relieve people of their belongings.)

Once a few guests have arrived, make introductions. Include full names, and pass along some tidbit of information that will launch a conversation, such as how Larry just got back from Tahiti, or Elizabeth just moved from Toronto.

In a small group it's easy to visit with everyone at once. Larger groups make it a little trickier to maneuver from person to person, but don't be daunted. Just take a few tips from experienced hosts: First,

memorize a joke or two before the party starts; it's a surefire way to keep conversations flowing and avoid awkward pauses. Second, remember that you can always jump-start a discussion by mentioning a current event—but unless you know your guests very well or you're ready to referee an argument, steer clear of controversial topics. Third—and most important of all—ask your guests about themselves, and always mention any good news you have heard recently about them.

The rest is easy. As you introduce your guests, offer them a beverage, fetch the first drink yourself, and point the way to the bar so they can help themselves to more. Pass a tray of hors d'oeuvres or just point guests in the direction of the food.

Sometimes you may need to jump-start
the conversation to get the party going.

If you are serving a meal, let your guests mingle for about an hour before you start the main event. Then simply announce that it's time for everyone to take a seat at the table or to head to the buffet.

When the last plate has been cleared, direct people to the living room, backyard, or front porch for coffee and conversation. Or simply push the dishes aside and stay at the table until everyone's talked out.

GAMES, ANYONE?

A party can be its own reason for being. If you're satisfied with serving people a meal and a drink and leaving it at that, fine. If, on the other hand, offering something beyond food, drink, and hospitality appeals to you, go for it. With a minimum of thoughtful planning you can treat your guests to an evening they'll remember for a long time to come. Here are some simple ideas to start you off.

Show slides. Everyone knows the old joke about being forced to watch slides of someone's summer vacation. Show yours anyway—but team them up with food, music, or a collection of souvenirs that everyone can appreciate. Or show old home movies and invite the "stars" over for a night at the flicks.

Hold a scavenger hunt. Select a holiday or special-occasion theme for the hunt. Divide guests into groups and give each one a list, a time limit, and a final meeting place. The group that acquires the most items on the list wins.

Play games. If it's a small group, pull out a deck for an impromptu game of poker. Or play charades after dessert.

PLAN PARTICIPATORY ACTIVITIES AS ICEBREAKERS. THEY BRING OUT THE LAUGHTER AND ADD TO THE PLEASURE OF A FESTIVE GATHERING.

Wine tasting

Buy wines of the same variety, such as several bottles of Sauvignon Blanc. Cover the bottles with paper bags or foil, and pour small amounts in each guest's glass. Discuss each wine, and take notes to remember which one guests liked best. Afterward, serve the wine with assorted cheese and crackers.

Prop swap

Each guest arrives wearing something to swap—a toy six-shooter, a fake tiara—that has a tall tale to go with it. During the evening, guests trade props (and tales) and get to know each other. Later, each guest regales the crowd with the story behind the prop he or she ended up wearing.

Secret ambitions

Ask your guests to write down on slips of paper what they would want to be if they could choose any profession. Divide the guests into two teams; have them take turns pulling the slips out of a bowl and guessing the owner of each ambition. Allow only three guesses before the owner must confess.

FINAL Tasks

—✳—

1 Try to **clean up** as you go, rather than leaving everything to

the end. **2** Set up a **busing station** in the kitchen, with a

trash can to hold plate scrapings, a cleared sink for rinsing, and counter

space for setting rinsed dishes. **3** **Start by collecting** the

trash and the recycling, then tackle washing, drying, and putting every-

thing away. **4** Count the **silverware,** glassware, and other

small objects before you take out the trash to **avoid tossing** away

any heirlooms. **5** To **simplify your next event,** keep all

your party gear in one readily accessible place. **6** **Label** each

storage box with its contents and note how many items it contains.

7 Be prepared for **overnight guests**—even unexpected

ones. Make them feel comfortable by setting out any amenities ahead

of time. **8** Arrange to return anything borrowed or left behind;

write **thank-you notes** for gifts and valuable assistance. ●

A Happy Ending

PAINLESS CLEANUP AND RECOVERY

* —— * —— *

The party's over. Sit down, kick off your shoes, put your feet up, and bask in the glow of the evening. Pat yourself on the back—you deserve it. You worked hard to make this event a big success. You're about to work a little more, too. You've still got cleaning up to do, and if a guest or two will be staying the night, you're still on the job as gracious host.

But don't let the party's aftermath stress you out. Address cleanup in the same organized, positive, and lighthearted way that you planned the gathering, and you'll breeze through it. If your remaining guests offer to help, by all means let them. Otherwise, make sure they're comfortably settled.

Decide which chores can wait until the morning, and which can't. Tomorrow you'll say good-bye to your overnight guests; later in the week you'll write thank-you notes and return borrowed items. And as life returns to normal, you'll have time to reflect on a party enjoyed by all, especially you.

CLEAN IT UP, PUT IT AWAY

JUST THE THOUGHT OF CLEANING UP AFTER A PARTY IS ENOUGH TO MAKE SOME PEOPLE SKIP ENTERTAINING ALTOGETHER. BUT THE TASK NEEDN'T BE BURDENSOME. ALL IT TAKES IS A FEW LABORSAVING STRATEGIES.

The simplest way to minimize post-party labor is to clean as you go. As you finish using a pot, wash it or pop it into the dishwasher. Run a load and put the contents away before your guests arrive. As you complete each task, wipe the countertop. Throw away trash as it accumulates. If you continue the clean-as-you-go approach into the party, handling the aftermath will be easier than you imagined.

A little forethought can save you hours of cleaning time. Put out plenty of coasters to shield your tabletops. Make sure that trash containers are abundant and easy to find, especially at large gatherings. Set up a busing station in the kitchen, with a trash can to hold plate scrapings, a cleared sink for rinsing, and counter space for setting dishes that have been rinsed.

STRATEGIC CLEANING

No matter how carefully you've prepared, once the party has ended there will be some cleaning up to do. Its extent will depend on the size and location of the gathering. A small summer get-together on the patio may mean just washing a few dirty plates and glasses. A large, raucous gathering in your living room on a rainy night may require mopping muddy floors, collecting bags of garbage, and washing several loads of dishes.

But even a houseful of cleaning will go quickly if you approach it strategically. For starters, put away leftover food and scrape plates clean. Then scout out situations that demand immediate attention, where something can be harmed, or can do harm, if left until morning—a red wine spill on your best white tablecloth, for example, or crystal candlesticks set within reach of a toddler.

If you're still wide awake, riding high on the evening's adventure, crank up some energetic music and go to it. But if you

Label Everything

Stocking up makes sense only if you can find everything when you need it. Keep track with carefully labeled containers. For permanent supplies, mark outer boxes with what's inside. For paper goods, plastic ware, and candles, count what you have as you put each item away, and mark the number on a sheet of paper taped to the outside of the box. Adjust the number whenever you use up items.

Put party items away where you're sure to find them the next time.

feel about as sprightly as the drooping flowers in the centerpiece, go to bed. The state of your home will look considerably less daunting after a good night's sleep.

step. Start in the living room and work your way through the party site, ending up in the kitchen. Whenever you see a spot on a piece of furniture, wipe it off.

The simplest way to minimize post-party labor is to clean as you go. As you finish using a pot, wash it or pop it into the dishwasher.

Don't remove anything from the party area until you've accounted for every piece of silverware and glassware, every napkin ring and candlestick—the world's landfills are crammed with family heirlooms last seen at parties. Then grab a large, heavy-duty garbage bag and move from room to room, dropping in trash. Follow the same path for recyclables. Along the way, pick up any stray glasses and plates and return them to the kitchen. Next, gather up dirty linens, pretreat the stains, and throw them into the laundry hamper.

A damp sponge, spray cleaner, and a little elbow grease will handle the next

Next, vacuum the floors, checking for any spills you've overlooked. Finally, return the furniture to its normal arrangement.

When you get to the kitchen, fill the dishwasher and run the first load. While it's running, wash, dry, and put away fragile china and crystal (when in doubt about whether something is dishwasher safe, clean it by hand). If you have a large collection of hand washables to dry, set an extra dish rack or two on large sheet pans, or cover the counter with towels and let the dishes drain there. When the last piece is dry and stashed away, give the counters and stove a once-over.

The bathroom shouldn't need more than light cleaning. Wipe the sink with cleanser and a sponge. Put dirty towels into the laundry hamper and hang up clean ones in their place. Empty the trash can, refill the toilet paper, and replace the tracked-up rug with a clean one.

Before you know it, your home will be just as clean as it was before the celebration —possibly even cleaner!

CLEANING SOLUTIONS

The aftermath of a party always includes a few complex cleaning tasks, but they're all manageable. Here are some common situations and a solution for each.

Water spots on furniture. Remove water spots on wood with a furniture-restoration polish. You can minimize the minor but unsightly marks and scratches with a dab of mayonnaise or vegetable oil.

Candle wax. When votive candles stick to their holders, put them, holders and all, in the freezer for 20 minutes, then pop each candle out by gently tapping the holder on a countertop. Use a plastic spatula to scrape wax from tabletops.

Wineglasses. For spotless glasses, wash them in warm (not hot) soapy water, rinse them in hot water, set right side up for five minutes on a towel-covered counter, then invert and let sit a minute or two before drying with a cotton dish towel.

Oversize pots and pans. If they're too large for the dishwasher or the kitchen sink, wash them in the bathtub.

Leftover food on plates. Push food off thoroughly with a rubber scraper, then rinse both sides of the plate.

Burned pots and pans. Add a few drops of dishwashing detergent and soak pots and pans in water for as long as two days.

If burned-on food remains after a long soaking, attack it with a steel-wool soap pad and plenty of elbow grease.

HOW TO STORE

Now that you've got your house back in shape, tackle the things that need to be returned or stored. If you follow the same procedures every time, you'll find that your next party will go more smoothly.

Start with your silverware, counting as you put the pieces away. Next, put the china pieces back in the cupboard, tucking rounds of felt, soft paper, or bubble wrap between the plates and saucers. Store your crystal on shelves where it can't be knocked off easily. (If you use some china and crystal only on special occasions, look in a housewares shop for padded boxes made specifically for storing breakables.)

You should put decorations that you will use again into boxes and label them. If space allows, dedicate a separate box to each theme, holiday, or occasion. It will be easier to find what you need next time.

For sturdy, secure storage, invest in durable plastic boxes with lids, available at hardware stores or large housewares outlets. File boxes are a less expensive (and only slightly less sturdy) alternative; you can buy these at an office-supply store.

STEPS TO PROTECT

Take protective measures to keep your party gear safe and in top shape. Before storing fine table linens or other textiles, launder them, wrap them in clean cotton or acid-free tissue paper, tuck in a few cedar blocks, and put them in drawers or

Rather than saving *all of the cleanup tasks for the end, collect used plates and cups and fill the dishwasher as the party progresses.*

acid-free boxes, away from humidity and moisture. Wrap breakables in tissue paper or bubble wrap and pack them in boxes; store the boxes on low shelves to minimize the risk of your dropping them the next time you pull them out. Try not to store anything where it could get damp; if you must stash a few boxes in the basement, wrap items in plastic bags before packing.

To simplify your next event, keep all your party gear in one readily accessible place. Set aside space in a pantry or closet to store items used only for entertaining. Put those you use most where you can find them quickly; if you need to stack boxes, put the heaviest ones on the bottom. If you can't keep everything in one place, at least keep like things together.

Remember, you don't have to make your place shipshape in one day. Cleaning up certainly isn't as much fun as the party was, but it shouldn't be such a chore that you never want to entertain again.

PREPARING FOR OVERNIGHT GUESTS

---✳---

WHETHER YOU'VE INVITED OUT-OF-TOWN FRIENDS TO STAY WITH YOU, OR FREE-FLOWING WINE HAS RESULTED IN AN UNPLANNED OVERNIGHT GUEST, ALWAYS BE PREPARED TO EXTEND YOUR HOSPITALITY.

Don't expect overnight guests to help with the cleaning. If they insist, by all means let them pitch in; otherwise, show them to the guest room, or if they're camping out in a common area, lead them to a cozy chair, hand them a cup of coffee or a sandwich, and let them relax while you prepare their quarters.

If you've invited your guests to stay beforehand, make their comfort a part of your overall party planning. You don't have to re-create your favorite hotel; just think of the small touches that make you feel comfortable and welcome away from home, and provide as many of them as your time, space, and budget allow.

If you have a guest room, make sure that it's always ready—that way, surprise visitors will feel welcome. Equip the guest room with a reading lamp, an assortment of books and magazines, pillows and blankets, a couple of towels and washcloths, and an alarm clock. Roll in an extra TV if you have one, and keep the closet clear

Even if they're unexpected, make overnight guests feel at home.

MAKING GUESTS COMFORTABLE

✳

ENTERTAINING OVERNIGHT GUESTS provides an opportunity to unwind and spend extra time with friends or family. Make your guests feel welcome and comfortable with a few thoughtful gestures. Prepare as much as you can before the party starts, while you're still feeling creative and up to the task.

Breakfast in bed *is a rare luxury for most people. Pamper your guests by bringing them a tray of store-bought pastries, juice, and coffee or tea.*

Create a welcome basket *with a few toiletries, bottled water, and a glass; and something extra such as a loofah sponge or a jar of bubble bath.*

Add a special touch *to the bathroom by arranging contrasting sizes and colors of fragrant soap on an unusual plate.*

Stack soft, plush *towels and set them out before guests arrive; it takes only seconds.*

Taking Notes

Recording the details of a party is a great way to keep track of what worked and what didn't. Jot down a few notes: who was there; the party's theme; the food and drink and how it went over; and whether the quantities—and the budget—were on or near target. The next time you entertain, you can make decisions based on your own recorded experience rather than hazy memories.

enough to accommodate a few days' worth of clothes. Add a basket filled with basic toiletries such as toothpaste, a new toothbrush, a comb or brush, hand lotion, and shampoo and conditioner (stock up on trial sizes at the supermarket).

THE THOUGHTFUL HOST

Even if you don't have a guest room, overnight visitors won't pose a problem if you plan ahead. Simply keep some extra pillows, towels, and blankets on hand, and decide what sleeping arrangements work best in your household. In most cases, visitors (especially unexpected ones) will happily bed down on the couch. But if you're an early riser or your pets are nocturnal wanderers, offer guests your room and sleep on the sofa yourself.

If your guests will be staying longer than one night, show them around the house. Explain how to use the TV and the VCR. Provide them with a key to

the front door. Offer the use of your hair dryer, your bike or transit pass (lending others your car can result in an insurance nightmare), street maps of your area, an umbrella, and a warm coat if it's needed. Show them around the kitchen, explain how the coffeemaker works, and point out the refrigerator and pantry you've fully stocked in their honor.

Whether guests are expected or not, try to anticipate their needs in a strange home. Provide a night-light so they don't have to grope their way to the bathroom, and leave an extra roll of toilet paper in plain sight. Warn them about the home-alarm system, quirky plumbing, and the front door that doesn't latch on its own.

If your guests will be staying longer than one night, show them around the house. Explain how to use the TV and VCR.

Let them know about strange sounds they may hear inside or outside the house, such as the sprinklers coming on at 6 A.M.

Once the last guest has departed, you'll need a few days to return forgotten items, write thank-you notes, and mail checks.

As with most of life's activities, the more you entertain, the easier and more fun it will be. With a little practice, you'll learn to recognize the pitfalls and be able to avoid them; you'll discover how to get maximum results with minimum effort; you'll even gain new perspective on being a guest yourself. With each event, you'll become better at simplifying entertaining.

CHECKLISTS AND RESOURCES

INFORMATION FOR PARTY GIVERS

✳ —— ✳ —— ✳

Maybe you balance work, family, and home chores with the precision of a circus juggler. But now you're throwing a party, and your workload has gone over the top. Don't worry. The following checklists and work sheets will keep time and effort to a minimum. Photocopy them to use again and again.

With everything on paper, you can evaluate your choices and decide whether you really have the time (or the desire) to do as much as you envisioned. That formal dinner party for eight might make more sense to you, your guests, and your pocketbook as a casual barbecue on the patio.

These lists will keep you on track as you choose the menu, shop for food and supplies, send invitations, and rally your support system (whether hired or volunteer). After the party, use the lists to critique your event. Add a few photographs, and you've got a springboard for planning your next party—and the start of your own entertaining resource library.

PARTY BASICS

DECISIONS TO MAKE NOW

※

THE KEY TO LOWER-STRESS ENTERTAINING IS STRONG ORGANIZATION AND A PRACTICAL ACTION PLAN. USE THIS CHECKLIST EACH TIME YOU ENTERTAIN TO RECORD YOUR DECISIONS AND TRACK YOUR PROGRESS.

INITIAL DECISIONS
☐ Business
☐ Pleasure
☐ Special occasion
☐ Just for fun
☐ Budget
☐ Location
☐ Date
☐ Time
☐ Theme

FIRST THINGS FIRST
☐ Make guest list
☐ Send save-the-date notices
☐ Send invitations (don't forget maps!)
☐ Take inventory
☐ Gather equipment
☐ Reserve rentals
☐ Make a schedule

FINDING HELP
☐ Professional services
☐ Volunteers

FOOD AND DRINK
☐ Select menu
☐ Map out a cooking schedule
☐ Make a shopping list
☐ Wash crystal and china

☐ Polish silver pieces
☐ Prepare linens
☐ Stock the bar

GETTING READY
☐ Make arrangements for kids and pets
☐ Shop for food and supplies
☐ Clean the house
☐ Decorate the site
☐ Rearrange the furniture
☐ Select games and activities
☐ Clear space for coats
☐ Arrange flowers
☐ Put on music
☐ Light candles and start fire

OVERNIGHT GUESTS
☐ Buy food for breakfast
☐ Ready bedroom and bathroom
☐ Set out amenities
☐ Coordinate morning-after plans

FOLLOWING UP
☐ Send thank-you notes
☐ Return rented and borrowed items
☐ Arrange return of forgotten belongings
☐ Pack decorations
☐ Store china and crystal
☐ Arrange for extra trash pickup

Preparing the Site

SETTING UP THE PARTY LOCATION

———— ✳ ————

FINDING THE RIGHT PLACE FOR YOUR GATHERING WILL INVOLVE A LITTLE RESEARCH AND A FEW ARRANGEMENTS. USE THIS CHECKLIST TO HELP YOU SELECT AND PREPARE THE PARTY LOCATION.

DECIDING ON A SITE
- ☐ Inspect site
- ☐ Request price estimates
- ☐ Visit at same time of day as event
- ☐ Count seating

Check details:
- ☐ Capacity
- ☐ Access for guests
- ☐ Hours of access
- ☐ Caterer restrictions
- ☐ Liquor restrictions
- ☐ Music restrictions
- ☐ Decorating guidelines
- ☐ Parking availability
- ☐ Extra fees
- ☐ Cleanup charges
- ☐ Insurance requirements
- ☐ Coat-check availability
- ☐ Air conditioning, heating
- ☐ Electrical outlets
- ☐ Sound system

ONCE SITE IS SELECTED
- ☐ Sign contract
- ☐ Pay deposit
- ☐ Arrange billing
- ☐ Note equipment and supplies to bring
- ☐ Draw up seating chart
- ☐ Arrange for rental equipment needed

AT RESTAURANTS
- ☐ Meet with manager and chef
- ☐ Select menu
- ☐ Choose wines
- ☐ Taste food and wine
- ☐ Make parking arrangements
- ☐ Make confirmation call

AT OUTDOOR EVENTS
- ☐ Prepare a rain plan
- ☐ Ensure insect control
- ☐ Check propane or charcoal supply
- ☐ Consider climate of site

Check details:
- ☐ Lighting
- ☐ Rest-room access
- ☐ Adequate electrical outlets
- ☐ Heaters
- ☐ Area for dancing
- ☐ Clear walkways
- ☐ Windbreaks
- ☐ Shade

DAY OF THE EVENT
- ☐ Arrive at least one hour early
- ☐ Ventilate room
- ☐ Finish decorating
- ☐ Create ambience
- ☐ Set out name cards

SUPPLIES CHECKLIST

GETTING READY FOR A CROWD

✴

EVERY PARTY WILL REQUIRE THESE ITEMS IN VARYING QUANTITIES. START WITH THIS LIST OF COMMONLY USED PARTY EQUIPMENT AND SUPPLIES AND EXPAND IT TO FIT YOUR ENTERTAINING NEEDS.

INSIDE

☐ Chairs
☐ Other seating
☐ Buffet table
☐ Dining table
☐ Bar
☐ Ice tub or cooler
☐ Coatrack

OUTSIDE

☐ Barbecue
☐ Charcoal
☐ Lighting
☐ Cooler chest

DINING AREA

☐ Cocktail napkins
☐ Tablecloths and napkins
☐ Place mats

☐ Plates (plastic, paper, or china)
☐ Flatware (plastic, stainless, or silver)
☐ Glasses (plastic or glass)
☐ Cups (paper, plastic, or ceramic)
☐ Serving platters and utensils

COOKING AREA

☐ Large pots and pans
☐ Cutting boards
☐ Coffeepot
☐ Hot plate

CLEANING SUPPLIES

☐ Paper towels
☐ Spray cleaner
☐ Dishwashing soap
☐ Dishwasher detergent
☐ Dishcloths
☐ Sponge
☐ Furniture polish

DON'T FORGET

☐ Extra extension cords
☐ Hangers
☐ Garbage cans and bags
☐ Ashtrays
☐ Coasters
☐ Serving trays

Good organization will keep stress to a minimum.

RENTAL CHECKLIST

ESSENTIALS AND EXTRAS FOR A BIG BASH

———— ✳ ————

RENTING IS A GREAT SOLUTION WHEN YOU ARE HOSTING A LARGE GROUP OR DON'T HAVE TIME TO WASH, DRY, AND PUT AWAY YOUR OWN EQUIPMENT AND SUPPLIES. USE THIS WORK SHEET TO PLAN YOUR NEEDS AND QUANTITIES.

TABLEWARE
- ☐ Tablecloths
- ☐ Napkins
- ☐ Salt and pepper shakers
- ☐ Dinner plates
- ☐ Salad plates
- ☐ Dessert plates
- ☐ Bread and butter plates
- ☐ Soup bowls
- ☐ Salad forks
- ☐ Dinner forks
- ☐ Knives
- ☐ Soupspoons
- ☐ Teaspoons
- ☐ Dessert forks and spoons
- ☐ Cups and saucers
- ☐ Creamers and sugars

SERVICE WARE
- ☐ Serving utensils
- ☐ Platters and trays
- ☐ Chafing dishes
- ☐ Large bowls
- ☐ Small bowls
- ☐ Coffeemaker
- ☐ Coffee carafes
- ☐ Punch bowl and cups
- ☐ Wine decanters
- ☐ Ice bucket

GLASSWARE
- ☐ All-purpose
- ☐ Highball
- ☐ Old-fashioned
- ☐ Shot glass
- ☐ Champagne
- ☐ White wine
- ☐ Red wine
- ☐ Water
- ☐ Dessert wine/brandy snifter

OUTDOOR EQUIPMENT
- ☐ Large umbrellas and stands
- ☐ Tents
- ☐ Heaters
- ☐ Canopy

LARGE-PARTY GEAR
- ☐ Tables
- ☐ Chairs
- ☐ Bar
- ☐ Coatrack
- ☐ Dance floor
- ☐ Stage
- ☐ Screens
- ☐ Large grill
- ☐ Large cooler chest
- ☐ Waiter trays
- ☐ Waiter stands

QUESTIONS TO ASK A CATERER

FINDING THE BEST PROFESSIONALS

— ✳ —

USE THIS LIST TO HELP YOU MAKE DECISIONS AND GUIDE THE CATERER'S EFFORTS. FOLLOWING IT WILL ENSURE THAT YOU DISCUSS IMPORTANT ISSUES. LATER, IT CAN SERVE AS A RECORD OF DECISIONS YOU'VE MADE.

◆ Who will order rental equipment?

◆ When will rental equipment be dropped off? When will it be picked up?

◆ Who will order flowers?

◆ Who will decorate tables?

◆ Who will arrange for valet parking?

◆ Do you have insurance?

◆ Do you automatically add a gratuity?

◆ Do you add a fee for hiring other services or ordering rentals?

◆ Will you staff and set up the bar?

◆ How many staff people will you need?

◆ Can you accommodate food preferences and special diets?

◆ What are your menu specialties?

◆ Do you recommend a buffet or a seated meal? What are pros and cons?

◆ Will you pass food around on trays or leave hors d'oeuvres on a buffet table?

◆ What are the options for dessert?

◆ Will you provide coffee service?

◆ What time will you arrive at the site?

◆ What is entailed in the cleanup? How long do you estimate it will take?

◆ Will you supply table linens? Please describe your usual selection. What are the options for colors and fabrics?

◆ Will you supply table decorations? Please describe your usual selection. What are the options?

◆ Will you supply dishes and utensils? Please describe your usual selection. What are the options?

◆ What kind of storage, baking, and preparation space will you need?

◆ How many electrical outlets will you need? What if there aren't enough?

PROFESSIONAL SERVICES

WHO'S WHO, ALL IN ONE PLACE

———— ✳ ————

IF YOU HIRE VENDORS OR GATHER FRIENDS TO HELP YOU, JOT DOWN NAMES, NUMBERS, AND VITAL STATISTICS. USE THIS SHEET NOW FOR QUICK REFERENCE; USE IT LATER TO PLAN PARTIES OR PROVIDE REFERRALS FOR FRIENDS.

PARTY PLANNER_____

_____

Phone number:_____

Price estimate:_____

Time of arrival:_____

Special needs:_____

CATERER_____

_____

Phone number:_____

Price estimate:_____

Time of arrival:_____

Special needs:_____

DECORATOR_____

_____

Phone number:_____

Price estimate:_____

Time of arrival:_____

Special needs:_____

FLORIST_____

_____

Phone number:_____

Price estimate: _____

Time of arrival: _____

Special needs: _____

GARDENER_____

_____

Phone number:_____

Price estimate:_____

Time of arrival:_____

Special needs:_____

BARTENDER_____

_____

Phone number:_____

Price estimate:_____

Time of arrival:_____

Special needs:_____

ENTERTAINER_____

_____

Phone number:_____

Price estimate:_____

Time of arrival:_____

Special needs:_____

KITCHEN HELPER_____

_____

Phone number:_____

Price estimate:_____

Time of arrival:_____

Special needs:_____

BABYSITTER_____

_____

Phone number:_____

Price estimate:_____

Time of arrival:_____

Special needs:_____

Menu and Presentation

MEAL ITEMS AND SERVING CONTAINERS

※

ONCE YOU'VE NARROWED YOUR CHOICES ON THE MENU WORK SHEET, USE THIS LIST TO WRITE DOWN YOUR FINAL MENU SELECTIONS. THIS WILL HELP YOU DETERMINE HOW MANY DISHES, GLASSES, AND UTENSILS YOU'LL NEED.

HORS D'OEUVRES

1._____

Serving dish_____

Utensils_____

2._____

Serving dish_____

Utensils_____

3._____

Serving dish_____

Utensils_____

APPETIZER

1._____

Serving dish_____

Utensils_____

2._____

Serving dish_____

Utensils_____

3._____

Serving dish_____

Utensils_____

MAIN COURSE

1._____

Serving dish_____

Utensils_____

2._____

Serving dish_____

Utensils_____

SIDE DISHES

Salad_____

Serving dish_____

Utensils_____

Starch_____

Serving dish_____

Utensils_____

Vegetable_____

Serving dish_____

Utensils_____

BREAD

Serving dish_____

Utensils_____

DESSERT

1._____

Serving dish_____

Utensils_____

2._____

Serving dish_____

Utensils_____

BEVERAGES

Wine_____

Stemware_____

Coffee and tea _____

Coffee service_____

Teacups_____

Liqueur glasses_____

MENU WORK SHEET

DISHES YOU CAN PREPARE IN ADVANCE

———— ✳ ————

USE THIS WORK SHEET TO THINK THROUGH YOUR MENU. STAGGER THE PREPARATION TIMES SO YOU HAVE A MIX OF COURSES TO MAKE IN ADVANCE AND RIGHT BEFORE THE MEAL. LIST UNUSUAL INGREDIENTS FOR SHOPPING.

Number of guests:_____

Buffet or sit-down meal?_____

Mealtime:_____

DISH:_____

Unusual ingredients:_____

_____

Advance preparation steps:_____

_____

Last-minute preparation steps:_____

_____

Total preparation time:_____

DISH:_____

Unusual ingredients:_____

_____

Advance preparation steps:_____

_____

Last-minute preparation steps:_____

_____

Total preparation time:_____

DISH:_____

Unusual ingredients:_____

_____

Advance preparation steps:_____

_____

Last-minute preparation steps:_____

_____

Total preparation time:_____

DISH:_____

Unusual ingredients:_____

_____

Advance preparation steps:_____

_____

Last-minute preparation steps:_____

_____

Total preparation time:_____

DISH:_____

Unusual ingredients:_____

_____

Advance preparation steps:_____

_____

Last-minute preparation steps:_____

_____

Total preparation time:_____

DISH:_____

Unusual ingredients:_____

_____

Advance preparation steps:_____

_____

Last-minute preparation steps:_____

_____

Total preparation time:_____

*Notes:*_____

_____

BAR CHECKLIST

OFFERING YOUR GUESTS' DRINK OF CHOICE

———— ✳ ————

A FULL BAR ISN'T NECESSARY, BUT THIS COMPREHENSIVE CHECKLIST WILL HELP YOU DECIDE WHAT TO SERVE YOUR GUESTS. USE IT TO CHECK YOUR CURRENT INVENTORY AND TO MAKE YOUR SHOPPING LIST.

SPIRITS
☐ Gin
☐ Vodka
☐ Bourbon
☐ Scotch
☐ Rum
☐ Tequila
☐ _____

CORDIALS/APÉRITIFS
☐ Pernod
☐ Vermouth
☐ Campari
☐ _____

WINES
☐ Champagne/sparkling wine
☐ White wine
☐ Red wine

DIGESTIFS
☐ Cognac
☐ Brandy
☐ _____

BEER
☐ Domestic
☐ Imported
☐ Microbrewed

MIXERS
☐ Tonic
☐ Club soda
☐ Cola
☐ Lemon-lime soda
☐ Ginger ale
☐ Orange juice
☐ Cranberry juice
☐ Margarita mix
☐ Tomato juice
☐ Bottled water (still/carbonated)

EXTRAS
☐ Lemons and limes
☐ Olives
☐ Maraschino cherries
☐ Superfine sugar
☐ Cocktail napkins, stirrers

EQUIPMENT
☐ Glasses
☐ Shot glass
☐ Long bar spoon
☐ Bar towels
☐ Corkscrew
☐ Bottle opener
☐ Cocktail shaker
☐ Blender
☐ Pitcher

SETTING THE STAGE

CLEANING HOUSE AND CREATING AMBIENCE

---✳---

STREAMLINE CLEANING TASKS AND ZIP THROUGH THE HOUSE WITH THE HELP OF THIS LIST. PLAN NOW TO HAVE A FEW ATMOSPHERIC ITEMS ON HAND AND IN PLACE. DON'T GO OVERBOARD—A FEW OF THESE TOUCHES WILL DO.

MINIMUM CLEANING
- ☐ Clean toilet and sink
- ☐ Replace bathroom rug and towels
- ☐ Vacuum floors
- ☐ Wipe countertops and table surfaces

FOR THE TABLE
- ☐ Centerpiece
- ☐ Name cards
- ☐ Decorative fruit and vegetables
- ☐ Table runner
- ☐ Baskets

AMBIENT LIGHTING
- ☐ Candles
- ☐ Candleholders
- ☐ Small lamps with extension cords
- ☐ Decorative lights

FLOWERS AND GREENERY
- ☐ Fresh-cut flowers
- ☐ Vases
- ☐ Garlands
- ☐ Wreaths
- ☐ Cut foliage
- ☐ Potted flowers
- ☐ Fresh herbs
- ☐ Potted houseplants
- ☐ Trees in containers

MUSIC
- ☐ Jazz
- ☐ Classical
- ☐ Rock and roll
- ☐ Salsa
- ☐ _____

FURNITURE ARRANGEMENTS
- ☐ Seating against the walls
- ☐ Chairs in groups
- ☐ Paths cleared
- ☐ Extra pieces stored
- ☐ Delicate objects out of reach

GAMES AND ACTIVITIES
- ☐ Board games
- ☐ Charades
- ☐ Videos
- ☐ Playing cards

Choose music that suits the occasion.

RESOURCES

READY TO PARTY? THE BOOKS, SUPPLIES, SERVICES, AND WEB SITES LISTED HERE SHOULD PROVIDE YOU WITH INSPIRATION FOR YOUR NEXT EVENT AS WELL AS EXPERT ADVICE AND THE EQUIPMENT TO HELP YOU CARRY IT OUT.

PUBLICATIONS

Bake and Freeze Chocolate Desserts
By Elinor Klivans
(Broadway Books, 1997)
A wide array of desserts to prepare in advance and freeze, then thaw in time for the big event.

Bon Appétit: 30-Minute Main Courses
(Random House, 1996)
A collection of easy-to-prepare dishes suitable for an entire menu or a quick meal.

Candles: Elements of the Table
By Sara Slavin
(HarperCollins, 1996)
Tips on selecting and arranging candles; includes the history and lore of candles.

The Complete Book of Mixed Drinks
By Anthony Dias Blue
(Harper Perennial, 1993)
This contemporary how-to book is a must for amateur bartenders; it includes a full range of cocktail recipes for every taste and occasion.

Crate & Barrel catalog
(800) 323-5461
Stylish housewares that are ideal for entertaining. The catalog offers a wide array of well-designed products at moderate prices for seasonal and special occasions.

Creative Greeting Cards: Personalized Projects for All Occasions
By Caroline Green
(Reader's Digest, 1997)
How to create one-of-a-kind invitations that express your unique style and your party's theme.

Dinner and a Movie Cookbook
By Claud Mann
(Turner Publishing, 1996)
A unique cookbook that matches menus with classic movies.

Flowers, Flowers!: Inspired Arrangements for All Occasions
By Paula Pryke
(Rizzoli, 1993)
For great instruction on flower arranging, the professionals turn to this book.

Linens: Elements of the Table
By Sara Slavin
(HarperCollins, 1996)
Photos of beautiful linens and great ideas for using them to your table's best advantage.

Mr. Boston: Official Bartender's and Party Guide
By Renee Cooper & Chris Morris
(Warner Books, 1994)
A timeless guide to mixing the perfect cocktail; contains all the classic drinks from martinis to margaritas.

Martha Stewart Living magazine
(800) 999-6518
A wonderful collection of seasonally inspired decoration, menu, and other ideas for entertaining.

Talking Dirt
By Jeff Campbell
(DTP, 1997)
A practical guide to efficient cleaning, with tips and information to make the inevitable easier.

Williams-Sonoma Casual Occasions
By Joyce Goldstein
(Weldon Owen, 1995)
Menus for a wide range of informal get-togethers, from backyard barbecues to a quiet dinner for two.

SUPPLIERS

All Occasion Tents
(800) 799-8368
Call for referrals to tent rental companies in your area.

Calyx & Corolla catalog
(800) 800-7788
Flower shopping has never been easier: Simply pick up the phone and order cut flowers, plants, or wreaths.

Fancy Foods Gourmet Club
(800) 576-3548
From smoked salmon to chocolate cake, this catalog has gourmet products to stock your pantry.

Kinko's
(800) 254-6567
www.kinkos.com
Stationery for invitations, name cards, or save-the-date notices. Buy supplies there, or use the store's computers and printers.

Orchard Supply Hardware
(888) 746-7674
www.osh.com
Perfect for garden and household needs; everything from hardware (such as lights and electrical cords) to decorating items (such as galvanized containers and tiki torches).

Pier 1
(800) 447-4371
Food, housewares, decorative items, and furniture from around the world; an ideal place to stock your party pantry or buy large cushions.

Pottery Barn
(800) 922-5507
Everything from couches to candles, from cases to corkscrews, from serving platters to napkin rings. Merchandise available from the catalog and stores nationwide.

Target
(800) 800-8800
Inexpensive, one-stop shopping for everything from glassware and folding chairs to seasonal decorations, paper goods, and storage containers.

Williams-Sonoma
(800) 541-2233
Find gourmet products by mail-order from the catalog or in Williams-Sonoma stores nationwide. You'll find everything from premade sauces and condiments to table linens and cookware.

ORGANIZATIONS
American Federation of Musicians
(212) 869-1330
Use this musicians' organization to find musical entertainers. Call the

headquarters' membership department for a chapter in your area.

National Association of Mobile Entertainers
(215) 491-4027
www.djkj.com
"Mobile entertainers" are DJs—hundreds of them working nationwide. Peruse the Web site or call the headquarters for a DJ in your area.

OTHER
The Glorious Art of Flower Arranging
By Valerie Arelt
(800) 752-6896
An easy-to-follow video that will help you create beautiful bouquets, handsome centerpieces, and other creative arrangements.

U.S. Department of Agriculture, Food Safety and Inspection Service
(800) 535-4555
www.usda.gov/fsis
This service provides information about food safety and cooking. Use it when you entertain or whenever you have questions about safe cooking methods.

THE INTERNET
Find more products, services, books, and recipes than you could possibly imagine. Using your favorite search engine, simply type in keywords such as "party services," "entertaining," "event planning," or "party menus." They'll lead you to rental companies, retail suppliers, booksellers, and even online magazines that can supply you with a wealth of advice—and some great recipes. Also try the following Web sites:

Beringer Vineyards
www.beringer.com
Beringer Vineyards offers expert advice on pairing food and wine, along with recipes that go well with suggested wines.

Robert Mondavi Winery
www.robertmondavi.com
Robert Mondavi gives ideas for entertaining with wine.

The Catering Connection
www.caterconnect.com
This nationwide referral service can assist you in finding a caterer in your region.

cybermeals
www.cybermeals.com
cybermeals lists thousands of restaurants on its delivery service site. Type in your location and pick from a menu when you want to order in.

Epicurious
www.epicurious.com
More than 6,500 recipes from Gourmet *and* Bon Appétit *magazines are at your fingertips here, along with cooking and wine tips.*

foodwine.com
www.foodwine.com
Award-winning site has sections on wine and gourmet cooking.

HomeArts
www.homearts.com
Here you'll find online versions of Town & Country, Good Housekeeping, Country Living, *and more.*

Hometown Online
www.hometownonline.com
The entertaining section of this online magazine includes articles on entertaining, easy party giving, and stylish decorating.

INDEX

ACKNOWLEDGMENTS

ADDITIONAL PHOTOGRAPHY: **Woodfin Camp** 40 Catherine Karnow. **FPG** 18 H. G. Ross; 24 Mike Malyszko; 81 David McGlynn. **Index Stock** 14 Rana Faure; 48 SW Productions. **International Stock** 12 Scott Barrow; 91 Klesenski. **Stock Market** 16 Jon Feingersh; 35 William Whitehurst; 67 Chuck Savage; 77 Craig Hammell; 129 Michael A. Keller. **Tony Stone Images** 20 Bruce Ayers; 32 Rosanne Olson; 52 Daniel Bosler; 62 Paul Souders; 84 Jamey Stillings; 87 Suzanne & Nick Geary; 88 Stewart Cohen; 110 Peter D'Angelo. **Uniphoto** 58 Terry Wilde; 82 Bob Llewellyn; 93 Tom Wolfe. **Westlight** 72 Japack. Author photo by Brian Pierce. SPECIAL THANKS: The publishers wish to thank the following people for their valuable help during the creation of this book: Desne Border, Nancy Carlson, Rick Clogher, Mandy Erickson, Ruth Jacobson, Cynthia Rubin, Carrie Spector, Patrick Tucker, and Laurie Wertz for editorial assistance; Gigi Haycock for help with photo styling; Pamela Korn for artist representation; Paul Rauschelbach for computing support; Sharon Smith for jacket design; Bill and Kristin Wurz for design assistance; Ty Koontz for indexing.